In the Beginning There Was Freedom

An Itinerary between Science, Philosophy, and Faith

GW00722327

Agincourt Books are edited and published by

Luigi Ballerini
Beppe Cavatorta
Gianluca Rizzo
Federica Santini

ISBN: 978-1-946328-25-0

AGINCOURT PRESS
P.O. Box 1039
Cooper Station
New York, NY 10003
www.agincourtpress.org

The publisher welcomes enquiries from copyright-holders he has been unable to contact

Michela Dall'Aglio

In the Beginning There Was Freedom

An Itinerary between Science, Philosophy, and Faith

Translated by
Thomas Haskell Simpson

Agincourt Press
New York, 2020

In memory of my sister, Daniela

Table of Contents

Introduction

In Dostoevsky's *The Brothers Karamazov*, Christ returns to Earth, is arrested, and is condemned to death for the crime of having brought misery to humankind by granting them, through his message, a freedom they neither desire nor know how to manage. Instead, "If we want man to be happy," the Grand Inquisitor decrees, "we must eliminate freedom."[1]

Another literary figure and symbol of innocent suffering, the Bible's Job, charges God with not saving good men from pain and death while the Earth has been "given into the hand of the wicked" and judges emit sentences devoid of justice. Job cries out in bitterness against God, "Cease then, and let me alone that I may take comfort a little, Before I go whence I shall not return, even unto the land of darkness and the shadow of death."[2]

Although separated by 2,000 years, Job and the Inquisitor both grasp a connection between suffering and freedom that calls God into question, doubting his beneficence, comprehensibility, and very existence. For Job, the problem is God's divine liberty to do with humankind whatever he wants. For the Inquisitor, the problem is human freedom, free will, which allows people to carry out the cruelest, most heinous acts. Freedom is an instrument with which God torments humankind and humans torment one another.

There is no question that evil summons both freedom and divine justice to its side, a fact that has always constituted the strongest argument against faith, especially faith in a God like the one represented in Judeo-Christian thought. How can a truly good God permit evil?

The presence of evil also overturns and undermines any human hope, even independent of faith, of finding meaning in the world. Over the course of history, many utopias, both religious and secular, have dreamt of freeing humankind from suffering, and their failure has provoked more death and misery than they thought to prevent. Their success in any case would not have spared us the griefs caused by nature, and even if we were to overcome disease and natural disasters, there would still be death to darken our horizon, leaving unfulfilled the dream of living in inexhaustible, unalterable wellbeing.

These are the considerations that have led me over the course of time to explore ever more deeply the subject of freedom, seeking first of all to understand what freedom means in political, ethical, and psychological discourse, and then to ask whether freedom has any meaning within a religious context.[3] This has led me to confront the question as to whether an infinitely good and omnipotent God would have conceived a world in which freedom has such a large and ambivalent role. What makes freedom so precious that—from God's point of view—it cannot be done without? The only answer I could come up with is that God cannot do without freedom. But again, why not?

At this point I seemed to find before me a kind of huge metaphysical puzzle with almost innumerable loose tiles to fit together. I was sure only that I must start out with the one piece I held in my hand: freedom.

The first step in the path traced out in this book is, therefore, a question— the first of many to follow—which, while simple in itself, is not simple at all in its presuppositions and the consequences it leads to: Can we free ourselves of freedom?

If freedom coincided entirely with free will, we could hypothesize the absurd and declare that it would be possible to eliminate freedom. If, as many have claimed, freedom is a sophisticated byproduct of the evolution of our brain and culture, that is if we are ourselves the originators of a freedom that has no foundation in objective reality extraneous to ourselves, then we could imagine a different evolutionary outcome resulting in a being similar to a human being, but not endowed with free will.

But if freedom does not coincide entirely with free will, if it is not something that we have *invented* or that springs from our brain like some sort of natural secretion, but rather is an quality intrinsic in reality, then eliminating it would cancel out reality itself.[4]

It is thus vitally important to ask where freedom comes from and whether it exists in and of itself. As philosopher Roberta De Monticelli observes, at its core the problem of freedom is metaphysical: does freedom "correspond to something in reality?" And if it does, "what exactly does it attest to the existence of?"[5]

The second step is to formulate a philosophical-metaphysical theory of freedom. This has been done by Luigi Pareyson (1918-1991). The first and fourth chapters of this book will dwell on his hypotheses. In the first chapter, I summarize his fundamental conception of the role of freedom in the first manifestation of being. Although I have sought to simplify as much as possible, the discourse may appear somewhat difficult to unravel. I hope the reader will not be discouraged: Pareyson's reasoning is vertiginous and can bring on a sensation of tipping into the abyss that features so prominently in his thought. The best way to enter into his philosophy is to abandon oneself to it, curious to see where it leads.

The third step in the research necessarily consists in a verification of the validity of the posited hypothesis. In our case, this means that if freedom is not a secondary attribute of life, a more or less illusory product of our mind or human history, but a generating factor of reality, then we must find its traces everywhere, in the physical as much as the metaphysical world, in the dynamics of the cosmos and biology. The third chapter is therefore dedicated to the action of freedom in the becoming of the Universe and life beyond the apparent *rigidity* of the laws of nature.

To return to the metaphor of the puzzle, at this point the pieces will have been put together, and now it is a matter of interpreting the image that has taken shape. What are the conclusions that may reasonably be drawn, if any, concerning the conception of the world and life, according to the initial premises we've established and the way the diverse factors at play interact one with another? Interpretation and its consequences, therefore, constitute the theme of the fifth chapter.

In closing, in the final chapter I have chosen to take up one interpretation in particular, one found in the Bible, since whether we like it or not, western thought has contended with the Bible and its conception of the human and the divine for two thousand years. Philosophy, anthropology, and science all have their roots in the Bible.

To write this book I have entered a fascinating world as a layperson, as one who quite literally stands outside the sacred precinct (that is, one who is *profane*) that any knowledge system constructs. Following the lead of unimpeachable scholars in many fields, I have been guided by the same passion that Etty Hillesum describes in her *Diary*: "There is an unquiet spirit in me that wants to draw from the world as many mysteries as it can."[6]

1. The Point of Departure: Being & Freedom

Philosophy begins with a question: why does something exist rather than nothing? Why do we, the world and everything that surrounds us, known or unknown, exist? Still more radically: Why does *being* exist? Over the course of time, the progressive development of consciousness has posed new problems for society to resolve, problems whose ethical, political, and moral implications have had major repercussions on the lives of individuals and society, presenting daunting challenges to human intelligence.

As a consequence, the original question at the root of it all, if not perhaps entirely forgotten, has been largely set aside, in part also because it has been substantially unanswerable. As philosopher Hans Jonas has remarked, "the modern critical development of philosophy now permits only questions that can be given demonstrable answers subject to rebuttal."[7]

Many philosophers have preferred to dedicate themselves to questions that seemed more urgent, more useful, or perhaps simply more manageable. Still, the problem of being and nothingness remains a cornerstone of philosophy and has neither faded in importance nor become less pressing; it continues to pulse subtly in the mind and every so often disturbs us acutely.

Among the philosophers who have refused to evade this exquisitely metaphysical question, which recent science has brought once again to the forefront, is Luigi Pareyson (1918-1991), who after a lifetime of reflection came to the conclusion that freedom is the origin of *being*, with the latter term taken to mean existence in all its material and spiritual forms.[8] He elaborated a conception in which freedom is real and inseparable from existence to such a degree that it is impossible to think of them separately. In other words, being neither can neither exist nor be comprehended without taking account of the freedom that belongs to it and constitutes its intrinsic dynamism. Pareyson thus maintained that the primary interest of philosophy must shift from the traditional opposition between *being* and *non-being* to the question of freedom.

Rather than *why does something exist rather than nothing?*, the foundational question should be *why does freedom exist rather than nothing?* Thus *being* and *freedom* are identical, although naturally, freedom does not exhaust all the qualities of *being*, as *being* encompasses other qualities as well, such as relationality and love.[9]

Hannah Arendt stated that God had introduced freedom into the world through humankind. For Pareyson instead, freedom is at the origin of any reality, and thinking radically about it can provide the key to problems such as Why is there being rather than non-being?, Who are we?, What is the meaning of the world? What is the origin of evil? and What is death? Facing life and its mystery without compromise, it is impossible to avoid the moment of existential anguish in which wonder distills into a single, ultimate, essential, absolute interrogative that encapsulates the very meaning of reality: *Why?*[10]

We begin therefore with this axiom: that being in all its manifestations is the result and expression of the dynamic force of freedom. Like molten lava in the Earth's core that formed and continues to shape and give life to the planet, freedom is the dynamic core from which reality springs, takes on form, and is nourished. Freedom is the innate law of life, without which nothing would or could exist. Freedom is primary: the absolute beginning is the decision to exist of a *will* capable of bestowing itself with existence. This will is absolute, abyssal, unimaginable, and incommensurable freedom.

Being and freedom coincide, arising together not out of nothing, but in opposition to nothingness, which represents the alternative—possible but unchosen—to the positive affirmation of the originary will. The first consequence of this is the unique origin of being and of nothingness understood as *ontological evil*. We will further explore this discourse in Chapter Four, but for the moment we will say only that *ontological evil* is evil in and of itself which comes before and beyond any concrete expression; it pre-exists humankind and reality. Inert and inactive in the dimension of the divine, it is not the absence of good, nor does it have its beginning in humanity. Instead it is the potent affirmation of a negativity that humans render active and concrete. Thus humankind is not the *origin* of evil; it is, however, *guilty* of the evil it realizes.

We can give the name of God to the originary will from which everything came to be. Let it be clear, however, that we intend our discourse to be philosophical rather than religious. In this case the noun *God* constitutes the premise of a mode of thought that accommodates the possibility of transcendence, but not as an object of faith.

Among the scattered notes gathered and put in order for the publication of Pareyson's *Ontologia*, there is one page—the very last—in the margin of which the philosopher wrote next to the word God, "What an unnerving being!" Among the many sensations we may feel when thinking of God, to be unnerved seems decidedly the most sincere and immediate. Who is God? Does God exist? And if God exists, what is he? Above all, is it possible to think of God, as we would like to do here, outside of the dimension of religion? *To consider God philosophically*, to consider the divine in the way one might conceive an idea as a hypothesis, in which God is not necessarily either the mechanism required to trigger the process of existence or the object of faith and veneration of religious cults. Is it possible—just as Karl Jaspers asked whether we might trace the origin of the world back to a transcendent being, and if so, if that being can be called God—to consider God freely, with an open mind, without prejudice, as "that which transcends the world and precedes it," and which could perhaps reveal the world's meaning?[11]

God is "not a primordial datum, but generative," which precedes being and institutes it.[12] God *is*, by virtue of God's own will to be, and is exactly what God wishes to be. This means, interestingly, that God is good neither by nature nor by necessity, but by choice: God is the affirmation of being, and that choice has become for us the paradigm of goodness. Thus God is not, properly speaking, *the good*, but rather "the chosen good". The divine victory against negation and nothingness is the establishment of being and life as good. Pareyson asks, "What else does 'God exists' mean if not that the good has been chosen *ab aeterno*?"[13]

Philosophy ponders God. Faith encounters God on a different level, different from that of "philosophy, understood as demonstrative inquiry and objective metaphysics."[14] The encounter with God is existential (and religious), while thinking about God is philosophy (or philosophical theology). These roads intersect but are independent; thinking about God can lead to faith and, vice versa, faith may drive one to subject to reason the tenets of one's belief. In each case, it is certain that philosophy can speak about God only by setting aside any pretense or intention of demonstration. This should be made quite clear in order to use the word *God* and its related vocabulary correctly and without equivocation, in a certain sense liberating God from the monopoly of the various religious faiths, in order to restore God to humanity. However intelligent, complex, and sophisticated the intuitions and conceptual constructions of the diverse cultures may be, God, if God exists, cannot be the exclusive monopoly of any single one of them. God must exceed all such bounds, must escape any human dream of possession or enclosing knowledge. In other words, if philosophy intends to reflect on God, it cannot make God a point of arrival, the result of an investigation, or an entity about which to *demonstrate* something. However firm the faith of any individual philosopher, God can only be "a premise, never the result of philosophizing."[15]

We've said that using the word *God* points to *transcendence*, and this word in turn asserts that "the world could have meaning".[16] If something extends beyond the world and its principle of necessity, we can imagine that it could be possible, within that transcendence, to locate meaning and an acceptable response to the fundamental question, "Why is there something rather than nothing?"

Thinking about freedom as the origin of existence rather than as something restricted to the realm of morality and ethics entails thinking about it in an absolute, radical sense. Human liberty together with what transcends it can be called *divine freedom.*[17] We grant this locution no specifically religious valence but refer to the primordial freedom that precedes any manifestation or specific derivation. The term clearly evokes the sort of symbolic language typical of myth, poetry, and of course religion, but it is necessary because it is the only way that allows us to speak of a reality that cannot be invoked by the lexicon of philosophical rationality.[18] Only through metaphor and allegory can we approach subjects such as the soul, evil, suffering, the *totally other*, the ultimate meaning of things, or the heart of reality (which obviously has no heart; the usage exemplifies the need to resort to metaphor).

To say that freedom is the source of everything means that at the origin of everything there is or was (the question of time, in this context, is purely a grammatical option) a choice, the absolute first choice: the choice by which being created itself by coming out of nothingness or by prevailing over the possibility of nothingness. Where nothing existed, something appears. It is a gesture—the first and only ever made—of absolute, unlimited freedom. It is the beginning behind which it is impossible to look, and yet one must try to do so in search of an explanation, in search of a possible meaning for existence that does not exclude hope. The primordial, originary choice, Pareyson asserts, is the first act ever carried out, that essential act of freedom by which being *bursts in*, establishes itself, and conquers negativity by dispersing nothingness.[19] Here is what happened: "In the universal void, suddenly and unexpectedly, a will willed itself and succeeded in bringing itself about."[20]

There is therefore a beginning, a Biblical *bereshit*. But even before creation, there is another, far more radical beginning, of which creation is merely a continuation. This is an action, a decision, a momentous, irrevocable choice made once and for all. Springing forth like water from its source, a will with no other cause or origin than itself brings about all reality, both material and immaterial, and all reality is indelibly marked by this origin. Without this act of freedom, life could not exist in any form whatsoever.

Such a gesture of absolute, unlimited freedom can be carried out only by *someone* autonomously able to decide anything whatsoever, even the choice to exist. Only one who can do this is truly, totally free. Any other form of freedom, including human freedom—the most evolved and sophisticated form we know—can be true, genuinely potent and even absolute, but can never be unlimited, because it is subject to a necessary condition. This condition may seem obvious or banal, but it is quite substantial: in order to be free, one must exist, and this is something we cannot decide for ourselves.

We can choose to die but not to come into the world, nor can we choose the conditions or place of our birth, our nation or family, our sex or physical characteristics. This fact significantly affects the borderlines of human freedom, which cannot ever be entirely independent from the freedom of others. Such limitation also offers us a first indicator of the deep ambiguity of freedom and perhaps all reality: we are free, but first we must be born, and we do so *entering into* a determinate situation—family, sex, nation, and so on. The condition we find ourselves situated in at birth simultaneously permits us our freedom and also constitutes the perimeter that establishes its boundaries.

The foundation of reality is not necessity, but the unlimited freedom of a *will to be* which solely underpins all reality. A concept that may strike us as far-fetched or totally unfounded may nevertheless be expressed quite concretely in the case of the Higgs boson (to be discussed in detail later), without which all matter in the Universe would disintegrate and vanish in an instant. Virtually all we know about the Higgs boson is that there is nothing keeping its perfect, incredibly delicate equilibrium in place. Nothing guarantees its constancy. It has been said that there is something mysterious and poetic in the fact that the entire Universe shares the same fragility and precariousness found in the life of every living thing.[21]

If the future of reality is by no means *necessary* or guaranteed, if what is could just as easily not be, if it is the fruit of a totally arbitrary, imponderable choice with no source but itself, then two fundamental consequences follow.[22]

First, without the security provided by a world determined by *necessity*, by an infinite succession of cause and effect, we should acknowledge the clearly unstable condition of the world and thus learn to manage it more prudently. Second, we might be able to look at the world in a different way, as a gift of freedom and liberality (it is not by chance that liberty and liberalism have the same root), and thus we might see ourselves, perhaps reassuringly, as buoyed up by positivity and love.[23]

Certainly, it generates a certain anguish, a *horror vacui*, to be aware that existence is precarious, not guaranteed by necessity, and encircled by a menacing *nothingness* that it could at any moment pitch over into. Not even the thought that the other face of absolute gratuitousness (understood as the lack of anything that belongs to us with absolute certainty) is an equally absolute generosity founded in what may be called love can free us entirely of this instinctive horror.

Just as nothingness could not exist without being and negativity could not exist without a positive will, in the same way the absolute gratuitousness of love could not exist without the precariousness that comes from the absence of certainty. It is a further sign of the ambiguity of the world that renders life contradictory and uncertain, the continuous push-pull between good and evil, joy and grief.

Ambiguity is an inevitable companion of freedom, almost a symptom of which freedom is the cause. Freedom has established good, providing space at the same moment for the possibility of evil, a potential one cannot avoid exercising because even refusal is a free act. Freedom thus reveals itself as contradictory, impregnated with necessity, the fount and opening for uncertainty. Reality, of which freedom is the matrix, carries within itself the very contradictions that scar it with a tragic, doleful trait of looming senselessness.

Necessity enfolds freedom without smothering it, because freedom is indeed given, but it exists actively in the act of being received. What seems a constraint may be observed, from another perspective, as a gift. In this way, necessity becomes freedom: one consents or not to the gift liberally given. Originary freedom, which gives and gives itself, stands before human freedom, which accepts or rejects. Originary freedom is so absolute as to be able to negate itself and reject its own origin. This represents the aspect of *passivity* in divine freedom and the unlimited aspect of human freedom. Original will neither constrains nor obligates; it accepts and accommodates the choices of humankind and life. God neither eliminates evil nor impedes mankind from committing it;

instead God stands at the border, the bulwark that protects being from nothingness and mankind from its choice of death.

A veil of ambiguity projects a certain shade even over divinity, because although in generating itself it has chosen the good, it has nevertheless rendered evil possible, the possibility divinity chooses against. The divine decision is founded exclusively on sovereign and arbitrary will, a will that wants only because it wants. Will is thus transformed into a source of anxious unease for mankind, which cannot reside on a secure foundation of deterministic necessity and can find hope only in a liberality that incessantly provides sustenance. Only freedom opposes nothingness and renders being steadfast:

> "all reality is nothing but a single act of freedom . . . everything can be summarized in this: pure freedom. Seamlessly continuous freedom is the very heart of the real, its fathomless profundity. . . it is an abyss, a bottomless depth."[24]

If this is so, if freedom is the law of life, the origin and nucleus of reality, then we must confront a very serious problem. We must find traces of its presence (or its action) all around us, even in the physical world. Do the processes that govern the dynamics of the world allow a greater or lesser degree of freedom to shine through? This is what we will now turn to.

2. Indications of Freedom in the Universe

"In the universal void, suddenly and unexpectedly, a will willed itself and succeeded in bringing itself about."[25] Thus Luigi Pareyson describes something truly impossible to say with the words of experience: the origin of being, the first step on the path at whose far extremity we stand asking ourselves the how and why of our life and—as here—of existence itself.

In the preceding chapter we presented the hypothesis that everything began with a will to exist so free and powerful that it willed itself and innervated all existence with freedom. Freedom thus is the very heart of reality. This assertion unquestionably posits an obscure origin, but the scientific hypothesis that the beginning of all things came about in a *quantum fluctuation of the void* cannot be any less obscure. The latter image is certainly as evocative and mysterious as Pareyson's.

Since science is quite aware of what it knows (a great deal) and what it does not (scientists tell us this too is a great deal; what we know, in fact, has made us recognize the immensity of our ignorance), it accompanies such assertions with a prudent adverb: probably. The probability in this case is very very high, because the mechanism of the scientific hypothesis of creation has been worked out in almost every detail. What is still missing, and may remain forever missing, is that very first triggering moment from which everything is derived. We have come so close to that moment that what remains still beyond view is tiny, almost a trifle: the question *why*.

There is another element that differentiates Pareyson's assertion from that of the scientists. The philosopher speaks of being that emerges victorious over nothing. Science speaks of a Universe that springs from something; exactly what we do not know, although there are some hypotheses, as we shall see. The language of science almost blends into that of philosophy when it speaks of *something between being and non-being*. Sometimes even scientists let themselves go and use the word *God* to refer to something we as yet have no other name for. Einstein did this when he expressed the wish to know the thoughts of God, and Stephen Hawking did so when he said we are at the point of entering the mind of God. This is not a question of faith, naturally, but of language: when the mystery becomes truly abyssal, it can only be spoken of with the poor tools we have at hand.

Everyone—scientists, philosophers, believers and non-believers—agrees that at the beginning there was something inexplicable. Whatever the origin of everything may have been, the hypothesis that concerns us here is that freedom played such a crucial role as to have left its footprint, something like a law or perhaps a specific dynamism in every aspect of the real. We must therefore seek to understand by what mechanisms, as far as we can know today, the Universe began, reality established itself and set to functioning, and life evolved. The question that most interests us in particular is whether everything is programmed. Is everything rigidly directed toward some end, or are there diverse possibilities, fortuitous events, possible choices, things that might not have been and yet came to be, no matter how improbable?

The origin of the Universe

The Big Bang. The expression used popularly today to refer to the theory that the Universe was born in something similar to an explosion was coined in the 1950s during a radio show by British physicist Fred Hoyle, who intended to mock the concept. He was, in fact, among the advocates of a stationary, eternal Universe without beginning or end. Hoyle was wrong, but his ironic destiny is that thanks to this episode his name will forever be linked to a theory he abhorred, which is now shared by scientists around the globe with the name given by Hoyle.

Today few doubt that our Universe was born and developed in a determinate moment due to an event science defines as *a fluctuation in the quantum void*. Like a wave that grows until it breaks through surface calm, bursting out to contend with other waves, something similar may have taken place in the primordial void, generating an infinite energy capable of generating life, time, space, and matter in a fraction of a millisecond.

Imagine a state of quiet when nothing is happening, in which there is nothing (or at least nothing of which we can have any knowledge). Suddenly the quiet breaks and something happens. An event of this type is called a *rupture in symmetry*. What broke the silence of nothingness was the absolute first rupture in symmetry, the "most important of all, the one between being and non-being. Something or someone must have disturbed the indolence of total symmetry, or the 'eternal nothingness'."[26]

Imagining a fluctuation is not very difficult; our world is full of liquids that move and fluctuate. Imagining nothingness, however, is nearly impossible. What is the void? For a long time it was thought simply to be a space, or a portion of space, with nothing in it. Today we know it's not so easy. Void resembles more a space in which there is something which we simply cannot see, not even with the most powerful microscopes. Absolute void does not exist in nature. What we call void is the quantum void, and it is full of particles and fields (which are diverse manifestations of the same material reality) that vibrate, move at astonishing speed, interact, disappear, or transform:

> "Even by isolating a region of space and extracting all particles, all radiation, all gravitational and electromagnetic fields, the zone would not be empty, but would be populated by continuous fluctuations that would manifest themselves as the production and annihilation of particles and anti-particles. We say, therefore, that quantum void is full of couples of virtual particles and anti-particles, impossible to observe directly, but with diverse indirect effects."[27]

Space-Time

The first person to think of the Universe as an empty space traversed by atoms of finite dimension was the Greek philosopher Democritus in the 5th century BCE. His insight was truly extraordinary, especially considering that he had no ability to observe matter smaller than the human eye could see; his idea was born purely from speculation. When Democritus tried to explain the void in which the atoms moved, he found no other way to define it than "something between 'being and non-being'".[28]

Democritus had to wait a long time to see his intuition confirmed, until the 20th century, when quantum physics demonstrated the granular nature of matter on an atomic and subatomic scale, and Einstein's theory of relativity cast light on the nature of space and time. In its first part, published in 1905 under the title: "Zur Elektrodynamik bewegter Körper" ("On the Electrodynamics of Moving Bodies"), Einstein elaborated the concepts of space and time in a new way, such that they cannot exist separately. Thus a new entity emerged: space-time. In our

Universe, time exists only in relation to space. There is no absolute time; rather, it *flows* differently according to its location in space. Beyond the three known, easily comprehensible dimensions available to our experience, there must be a fourth one, time, which does not exist in itself but only in relation to space, of which it is somehow a property. What this means in concrete terms is that simultaneous events do not exist in our Universe:

> "Our 'now' exists only here," such that "saying 'here and now' makes sense, but saying 'now' to designate things that 'are happening now' throughout the Universe makes no sense. It's like asking whether our galaxy is 'above or below' the Andromeda galaxy."[29]

The most notable consequence of space and time being so tightly woven one into the other is the fact that time could not have existed before space. It is senseless to ask what there was before the Big Bang because there is no "before" when there is no time.

In 1915, ten years after having published the theory of special relativity, Einstein released a second part known as the *theory of general relativity*. Described either by Lev Landau or Max Born as the most beautiful of all theories, it represents an awesome "mental image of the world", through which the great physicist managed to resolve the incongruencies between his idea of the new physical entity of space-time and knowledge of the force of gravity.[30]

Isaac Newton imagined space as flat and stable, but Einstein hypothesized that the mass and energy that pervade the Universe can modify the geometry of space-time, which moves, flexes, and curves like a "giant flexible mollusk" (the metaphor is Einstein's) that encompasses us.[31] There is no mysterious force that attracts planets to wheel about the stars or makes apples fall from trees; rather, planets run straight in a space that curves and captures them, as though they were marbles whirling in a funnel.

The gravitational field—space—pervades the whole Universe, and what seems the void to us is in reality an extremely rapid vibration of particles created and annihilated, a vortex between being and non-being.

Democritus was right, "and today, in an imaginary dialogue with him, we can claim to have isolated his 'atoms' and identified their diverse characteristics, and confirm that the 'continuous movement' he described closely recalls the continuous exchange of particles impacted by the elemental forces."[32]

The end of symmetry

Even when simply hypothesizing the void as a field of interaction where forces and particles are continuously created and annihilated, or when we imagine the Big Bang as provoked by a quantum fluctuation in a primordial void, we are making allusion to something that exists/happens *before* the Universe that we know could emerge.

What could this be? The theory of relativity presumes that there is an energy over which the physical laws we know have no sway. We even lack the words to speak about it: is it a place, a time, a state? Suddenly and without knowing why, something we imagine as a fluctuation in the void ruptures the quietude of symmetry, the equilibrium between being and non-being, between something and nothing.

A choice takes place during this rupture in primordial symmetry, a shift in balance in favor of being; an event, something different from what there was before, something that might not have happened but did. And the consequences would be immense.

We recall the other version of the same story: In the beginning, a choice provokes an event; a will willed itself. As we have already said, these are different words for the same insight. Therefore, at the very beginning of the beginning—hypothetical but plausible—of our Universe, there is a dynamic of freedom in play. It is indeed difficult to imagine that something took place in the face of the possibility that nothing might take place without making recourse to something like freedom. The alternative is to resort to the idea of an ineluctable necessity, as though the Universe were a baby that, once conceived, barring misfortune cannot help but be born. The hypothesis of a strictly deterministic Universe, however, presents diverse problems and seems contradicted by experience, for which reason it has been substantially abandoned by science, at least in its most rigid form.

No one knows what sparked the disturbance that broke the quiet and set to spinning the machine that has brought us here. It feels highly significant and fascinating to know that we owe our existence to a rupture, an imperfection without which we would most probably never have come to be.

Symmetry reigns in the Universe and the world around us, but it is not and could not be total. If it were, everything—matter and anti-matter, being and non-being—would balance perfectly. There would be absolute calm in which nothing could happen. Fortunately, "symmetry indeed exists in nature and it governs the whole, but this symmetry is never perfect: this, we may say, is the greatest mystery of all."[33]

In the first three minutes of the Universe, ruptures in symmetry follow vertiginously one upon another, as particles and antiparticles appear and disappear without pause. For a few instants, chaos took over, and in that gap the Universe may have explored all the infinite possibilities of existence. Many Universes may have been formed and annihilated in milliseconds. We know however that at least one of them survived: the one we live in.

The history of the Universe

What do we know of our Universe? We know that it hasn't existed forever, that it is not eternal, immutable, or infinite. We also know that it has three spatial dimensions and one temporal one, is immense in size and continues to expand at a growing velocity (this last a recent discovery). It was born approximately 14 billion years ago from an initial point, and all that exists—galaxies, stars, planets, and everything they contain—is fruit of its evolution.

The Universe, however, is not only a space; it is also a history, a successive concatenation of events. Since it had a beginning, it will also have an end, but we aren't able to say how that might unfold.

It could continue to expand, becoming ever colder and emptier because the galaxies are moving away one from another at increasing speed. This phenomenon has led some to imagine the existence of a dark energy able to oppose the force of gravity, which would otherwise tend to draw the galaxies together. With unlimited expansion, everything will end in utter frigidity.

If, on the other hand, after having reached a certain peak of expansion, the force of gravity overcomes the force pulling the galaxies apart, then the Universe will slowly collapse into a single point, incredibly dense and incredibly hot. And then a new Big Bang could start the whole merry-go-round once again to spinning. But if the dark matter pulling against gravity provokes further expansion, the Universe could fragment into many pieces.

Still another possibility cannot be excluded: the Universe could be the interior of an immense black hole of such proportion that its density would be diluted to the consistency of water, which would permit the existence of a three-dimensional world like ours. A fascinating hypothesis.

According to the most recent cosmological theories, the Big Bang created only pure energy. When time was equal to zero (t=0), the Universe must have had a radius point of zero and infinite heat and mass. The first fractions of a second of its history are impenetrable to us: this was the Planck Era, the time between t=0 and t=10^{-43} seconds, about which we cannot know anything because it is subject to physical laws inaccessible to us. This infinitesimal fraction of time represents a numerical limit established by Planck's Constant, which determines the smallest possible measure we can divide a physical entity into (a *quantum*); in this case, space-time.

The mystery of the origin is hidden behind that infinitesimal portion of time, and we shall leave it there undisturbed.

The Universe evolves

We have said that before the Big Bang, when the decision to be or not to be had not yet been made, we can imagine the initial object like a single point with no dimensions, a sphere of zero radius, with infinite temperature, curvature, and density. Infinite density signifies infinite temperature and thus infinite energy. This energy caused the sphere to expand at a velocity impossible in the Universe we know; far superior to the speed of light, such that in a single instant it acquired macroscopic dimensions, a thousand times smaller than its dimensions today.

To explain this phenomenon, it has been hypothesized that the Universe may have undergone a kind of propulsion, an extraordinary acceleration that provoked an extremely rapid exponential growth, called inflation because its dynamics resemble the homologous economic process of increasing prices.

The theory of inflation, or the inflationary universe, as scientists prefer to call the Big Bang theory, was proposed in 1979 by physicist Alan Guth to explain the uniformity found throughout the Universe, which was difficult to reconcile with the idea of an initial explosion and an incredibly rapid expansion of a myriad of events. Guth thought that such a condition could be achieved only if something had made the Universe inflate in all directions at once, thus maintaining its uniformity everywhere. In this way, "any irregularity present in the Universe would be smoothed out by the expansion, the way the wrinkles in a balloon distend when it is inflated."[34]

Thanks to this mechanism the Universe is homogeneous, has no center, and is not headed in any particular direction. As a consequence, the laws of physics we recognize are valid everywhere, even a million light years away from where we stand. After the discovery of background cosmic radiation (a residue of the energy produced by the first expansion) that confirmed the theory of the Big Bang, the inflationary hypothesis is now shared almost unanimously in the scientific world.

The instants that precede the Planck Era (10^{-43} seconds) are inaccessible to us, available only to speculation, but the traceable history of the Universe and its evolution begin from that moment. The steps in the chronology are disorienting to say the least: from 10^{-43} seconds to 10^{-35} seconds (some say $10^{-32,}$ but as non-experts it's wiser not to put too fine a point on it, since the differences are infinitesimal), then 10^{-11}, 10^{-10}, 1 second, 3 minutes, 380,000 years, 300 million years, 9 billion years, and 13,7 billion years (that is, up to today, more or less).

The small discrepancies, on the order of fractions of a millionth part of a second, found between one study and another in the chronological subdivisions of the phases of the first three minutes of the Universe, testify more to the rapid progress of our knowledge than to any confusion in scientific opinion. A recent case is the discovery of the Higgs boson, which solidified the Standard Model of particle physics (which we will soon turn to) and will certainly alter many important details in physics textbooks to come.

According to the theory scientists call GUT (Great Unification Theory), at the moment of the Big Bang, the four known forces must have been a single unified force.[35] For a period of microseconds, between 10^{-43} and 10^{-32} from the Big Bang, gravity, the electromagnetic force, and the two interactions known as the weak and strong nuclear force, must have been some sort of superforce, still little understood. The Big Bang produced an immense force, and for a tiny fraction of time the Universe was pure energy: for the unimaginably small duration of the inflationary era, everything is energy and potential.

To end the Planck Era, first the force of gravity separates out from the larger force; at 10^{-35} seconds the strong nuclear interaction and the electroweak interaction separate one from another; in the next fraction of time the electroweak interactions splits into the electromagnetic force and the weak nuclear interaction. At this point the bases of the Universe we know are established.

The separation among the forces permits the formation of the fundamental elements of matter, quarks and anti-quarks, and at the same time, for reasons still unknown, the equilibrium between matter and anti-matter is broken. A minimal asymmetry, on the order of one part in a billion, is sufficient to bring about matter. This was the first of many great strokes of luck that led us to where we are today. In fact, if symmetry had not been broken ever so slightly in favor of matter, particles and anti-particles would have annihilated one another, continuing to produce photons rather than an immense Universe capable of producing stars, galaxies, and infinite celestial clusters.

The forces in play

The force we have known for the longest time, gravity pervades the entire Universe and keeps everything under control by diminishing distances. It is the weakest of the forces and simultaneously active and passive: everything that is attracted in turn attracts. Gravity functions on the level of large bodies but is virtually irrelevant on the level of sub-nuclear particles simply because they are so small. Although we have known quite a bit about gravity for a long time, it continues to withhold secrets: as late as 2015, fully a hundred years after Einstein had postulated them in his theory, gravitational waves were finally witnessed in action.

Electromagnetic force received its name when Scottish physicist James Clerk Maxwell realized that electric and magnetic forces were actually different manifestations of a single force. Electromagnetic force governs many phenomena we observe in nature: it binds matter into solid bodies and atoms into molecules by making electrons circle atoms without flying off in all directions.[36] It is electromagnetic force that "makes chemistry work and thus living matter. This is the force at work in our brain's neurons, carrying information on the perceptible world. Electromagnetic fields generate the friction that stops rolling and sliding objects, allows parachutists to land safely, turns the motors of internal combustion engines, lights lamps, and allows us to hear the radio, etc."[37] Further, it is thought today that the weak nuclear interaction, which permits nuclear fusion in stars and is responsible for radioactive decay, may also be bound to electromagnetic force in a force called electroweak.

The final known force is the strong nuclear interaction, which holds quarks together within atoms. Like the weak nuclear force and in contrast to gravity, the strong nuclear force plays a role only over infinitesimal distances (billionths of millionths of centimeters).

The infinitely small

The four forces, which scientists attempt to trace back to an initial super-force, have shaped the Universe. But what are these forces really, and most of all how is it possible for a force to produce matter? In truth what we call forces are the effects of *mediating* particles of the forces on other types of elementary particles. . . . The discourse is getting complicated, so to get oriented the moment has come to introduce the Standard Model of Particle Physics (in brief, the Standard Model), the quantum theory that describes particles and matter and the forces through which they interact (except for gravity, which, as we've said, is not relevant in miniscule dimensions).

As of today, the Standard Model is considered the most efficient instrument for describing reality at an atomic and subatomic scale, and has been repeatedly confirmed in experimental observation. Its most recent, extremely important confirmation was the discovery of the Higgs boson, which took place at CERN in Geneva in 2012. This boson is fundamental because it is what gives mass to all the others.

According to the Standard Model, all reality, from superclusters of galaxies to ourselves to bacteria, are composed essentially of a dozen particles (and an equal number of antiparticles) of two diverse types: those that constitute matter such as quarks and leptons (the most well-known of these is the electron), and those that mediate among the forces (such as the photon).

The particles that constitute matter are categorized as fermions, so named in honor of Italian physician Enrico Fermi, because they share certain characteristics; in particular, they obey the *Pauli exclusion principle*, meaning that they cannot simultaneously occupy the same space.

The mediating particles of the forces, on the other hand, are called bosons, because they obey the Bose-Einstein principle, meaning they can coexist simultaneously in the same space. The most well-known boson is the photon, the mediator of electromagnetic force.[38]

Long hypothesized and necessary to the functioning of the Standard Model, the boson most recently confirmed experimentally is the Higgs boson, a scalar particle that confers mass on the other particles.[39] The hypothesis of its existence was born from a fundamental problem: since all particles are born without mass, it was natural to wonder where massive particles came from, and how to explain the huge difference in mass among the different particles. First formulated in the 1960s and finally demonstrated in 2012, the hypothesis predicts that in a time equivalent to 10^{-11} after the Big Bang, a field something like dense molasses filled the Universe, such that particles were unable to move rapidly and freely. As they began to attract and combine one with another, they acquired mass according to the interaction that took place within the field; the stronger the interaction, the heavier the particle became. The quantum excitations in this field are the Higgs boson (in quantum mechanics, particles and waves are equivalent).

The Higgs field still pervades the Universe in every part, keeping it massive. The question scholars are asking now is: will it always be so? Do we have any guarantee that the Higgs boson will continue its labor and matter will not suddenly disaggregate in a flash of light? After all, only the photon, which is immaterial, is so small as to slip through the mesh of the Higgs field without interacting.

It's an unnerving question, and has prodded physicists to apply a phase diagram to the Higgs boson to attempt to locate it.[40] Three zones appeared in their experiments, three possibilities: if the boson is located in a certain band, it has absolute stability, meaning that absolutely nothing happens, and the Universe cannot exist because there can be no quantum fluctuation to activate it. If it is located in another particular band, a situation of absolute instability arises, whether nothing holds together and everything immediately collapses. The Higgs boson, it turns out, is located in a third band, a band extremely close to the other two and extremely small, called *metastability*.

Illustrating this diagram during a conference, physicist Guido Tonelli, director of one of the two experiments that led to the confirmation of the Higgs boson (the other experiment was directed by physicist Fabiola Gianotti), made the observation:

"It' a curious thing, it seems almost as though our human condition as fragile beings is shared by our whole Universe. Our whole Universe, as far as we know, is in a condition that is a bit in equilibrium between stability—total boredom, no evolution, a flat Universe—and instability, a Universe that dies immediately, disintegrates, finishes. We are here to tell the story of this Universe which has lived for 13.7 billion years in this condition of precariousness very similar to the human condition."[41]

The Universe is expanding

At this point, having survived the first instants in the life of the Universe and having identified the forces in play, we can return to the history of the Universe in its further unfolding.

Inflation (which, incidentally, may have been set off in the Higgs field), the phenomenon that began at 10^{-37} seconds from the Big Bang, with an infinitesimal duration (it would have been complete by 10^{-32} seconds), would have been sufficient to double its extension every 10^{-37} seconds, "as though fleeing from itself with itself."[42] In this phase the Universe presents itself as a broth or foam of indefinite particles devoid of mass called *exotics*.

Thanks to the Higgs field that grants them mass, the particles begin to attract one another, forming the first atoms; quarks gather themselves into threesomes and begin producing neutrons and protons. The Universe swarms with particles and antiparticles, with an infinitesimal predominance of the former, as we've said. Particles of matter and antimatter begin to clash among themselves and a gigantic phase of annihilation begins, in which antimatter is virtually destroyed by matter (why antimatter disappeared remains a mystery). Now the Universe is a dense magma of matter in which temperature diminishes as the particles lose energy, moving more slowly and interacting less.

Finally, at three minutes from the beginning of everything, temperatures have dropped by a billion degrees. Protons and neutrons manage to approach one another at a distance that permits the engagement of the strong nuclear interaction, which as we said acts only at tiny distances and opposes the force of gravity that would have crushed them together.

Thanks to primordial nucleosynthesis (that is, the production of light elements) the first hydrogen nuclei (helium and lithium) form, but they are extremely unstable and are quickly annihilated. The Universe changes in appearance again and now resembles a dense fog of photons, electrons, protons, and neutrons. Photons are still trapped in this density and cannot escape, which is why the Universe is dark. At this point the Universe has existed for three minutes. It will take another 300,000 years, approximately, for temperatures to drop enough (about 10,000 degrees) to allow matter and radiation to cool enough to reduce particle collisions and allow the formation of stable atoms.

Finally, since atoms are neutral, photons interact very little with them and can begin to travel freely in the Universe, which is transparent to electromagnetic radiation. This is the moment of "And then there was light", about 380,000 years after the beginning of everything. Next, for approximately a million years, the Universe is pervaded by clouds of neutral gas composed of hydrogen and a small amount of helium, which become more dense due to the force of gravity. These clouds are the nursery gardens of the stars, which enjoy an extended infancy: it takes hundreds of millions of years for the first stars and proto-galaxies to form out of the clusters of hydrogen and helium; estimates guess at between 200 and 600 million years. The Milky Way forms when the Universe is slightly less than nine billion years old, and shortly thereafter, perhaps four and a half billion years ago, the solar system takes shape. On the temporal scale of the universe, everything else is current events.

Freedom and necessity in the Universe

All of this is quite fascinating, but does it tell us anything about the topic we're interested in, the theoretical foundations and function of freedom? Can we say that freedom plays a role in the life of the Universe, in its evolution, and in the dynamics that led to its existence? It seems to me that we can answer yes.

If freedom, as Kant says, is the faculty of being able to provide an absolute beginning for an action, no beginning can be called more absolute than that of the Universe. If something happens that is neither obligatory nor necessary, something that *is* but could equally not have been, then that thing happens by virtue of freedom, and the thing expresses that freedom.

The condition of our Universe, it seems to me, is precisely this. No motive has turned up at this point in history that would lead us to think of the Universe as an inevitable result. Its initial evolution resembles less a deterministic event than an unlimited exploration of its intrinsic potentialities. The Universe makes its own laws out of itself, verifying the possibilities of matter by testing and eliminating. Everything we know of the Universe up to this point offers comfort to the idea that some form of freedom was woven into its existence from the beginning.

Clearly, however, we cannot deny that in some way and to some degree, the concept of necessity also pertains to the order of the Universe. We cannot deny this necessity due to our own logical induction: we are here, and there is nowhere but here we could be. Our existence, after all, poses some very precise limits on the Universe, because we can only live in a Universe made exactly like this one. If the origin of the Universe was absolute freedom, such that the originary vibration led to the thinking beings we are, many indispensable steps were required to take place exactly as they did and in no other way down to the tiniest detail.

From gas to matter

The first step was the passage from an extremely light substance, such as the gas of hydrogen and helium that composed the primordial universe, to the large, heavy atoms that we are made of and that constitute the world we live in.

Contemporary cosmology has by now thoroughly reconstructed how that passage must have taken place. When because of gravity a molecular cloud of interstellar gas and dust collapses in on itself, it gets hotter and hotter, and at the end of a process lasting millions of years, it leads to the birth of a star. Stars have different destinies depending on whether their mass is of small, medium, or large dimensions. Some, at the end of a life lasting approximately 10 billion years, explode in an instant—for the briefest instant they become extremely bright and are known as Supernovas—and scatter through the Universe the matter produced in their interiors by nuclear fusion. First comes carbon, the basis of life, then in successive phases come iron, uranium, and gold. These stars are essential, because they furnish the material that everything is made of, including what is needed for the formation of other stars. On the other hand, medium-sized stars such as our Sun or still smaller ones undergo a period of stability lasting a few billion years, and then after having consumed their fuel (helium), they expand, expel their internal gases, and transform into white dwarfs, after which they die.

Obviously, it takes a great number of extremely massive stars to produce the quantity of matter that exists in the Universe, and a great number of galaxies are needed to accommodate the number of massive stars required. All this can happen only in an immense Universe that is old enough for things to have had time to evolve. Our Universe is indeed immense—finite, but immense—and sufficiently old to have formed galaxies, stars, planets, and, ultimately, a habitat adapted to our appearance on the scene. Only an extremely improbable sequence of events, and an infinity of astonishingly fortunate circumstances, have brought about this "first-class wonder".[43]

Necessary bonds

Certain universal constants of physics speak of very tight bonds, such as Newton's universal constant of gravitation, Coulomb's electrostatic constant, the speed of light in a void, and Planck's constant. We do not know why these constants have the exact values they do, but we know that if they were only slightly different, we wouldn't be here.

If for example the force of gravity was only slightly greater than it is, the Universe would not have expanded and cooled enough, whereas if it were weaker, neither stars nor other solid bodies would have formed out of gaseous clouds. The force of gravity acts in three-dimensional space, balancing planetary movement such that the planets complete elliptical orbits around a star without spiraling into it, but at the same time they remain hooked into their orbits without wandering off, lost in the Universe. If space were in only two dimensions, no organism would have the depth to accommodate internal organs; no digestive system, for example. In sum it is clear that even minimal variations in many different parameters would have been sufficient for the Universe to evolve in such a way as to make our appearance impossible.

Let's take our solar system. Here too we find various particular circumstances without which our planet would have never evolved to permit life. Our star, the Sun, is a medium-sized star in roughly the middle of its life cycle, in what's called a *stable phase*, in equilibrium between the forces of gravity and radiation. It should remain in this condition for another four or five billion years, then theoretically will follow the destiny of other stars in its category, expanding until it encompasses the Earth and then becoming a white dwarf. We have time, but the time is finite. The important thing for us today is that it is a star of a certain type that burns with a certain regularity, and has done so for enough time for us to develop and evolve on one of the planets in its system.

Finally, the Earth. In our solar system there is a very small zone considered inhabitable, where water can exist in its liquid state, and that is exactly where we find ourselves, assisted in maintaining our stability by the gravitational effect of our gorgeous and large (just large enough) satellite, the Moon. The chaotic and pyrotechnic dance of the beginning has become, in our system, a harmonious, calibrated waltz, just perfect for us. Our path on the Earth, as we shall see, has been a long one, despite seeming very fast and ever faster compared to the first ten billion years of the Universe, and this path too will have its pauses and sudden leaps.

Astrophysicists explore the Universe in every direction with ever more powerful instruments in search of solar systems like ours where they hope to find planets like Earth. They are finding quite a few at inconceivable distances. It is possible that forms of life similar to those on Earth have developed somewhere else, just as it's possible that different forms of life exist, types we cannot imagine. However it may be, we are the certain proof that there is at least one planet in the Universe where intelligent life exists, and for this to be possible there had to be an immense Universe filled with energy and creativity, and old enough to have witnessed many complex concatenations of events. Whatever interpretation one might wish to make of this fact, scientists, philosophers, and everyone else needs to take account of it, asking, like the prehistoric intellectual in a famous comic strip, "Who are we? Where do we come from? Where are we going?"

The freedom of matter

The freedom expressed in the spectacular creativity of the Universe is the same that flourishes in the fleeting indeterminacy of the infinitely small, a world difficult to understand and governed by rigorous law.[44] In the subatomic world, everything is relative and nothing is predictable. An indeterminism reigns that we could interpret as a manifestation of the specific form of freedom that pertains to matter. We could say, that is, that freedom is one of the physical laws of the subatomic world. However we choose to look at it, it would be a mistake to deny that in the indeterminism of the infinitely small the road opens to possible and potential dynamics of freedom. With this in mind, and within our limits as laypeople, let's take a glimpse into the complex field of quantum physics.

The true nature of reality

The Twentieth century was an extraordinary period for science, witnessing the emergence of two theories that revolutionized physics and modern life. One is Einstein's theory of relativity, with its surprising vision of the nature of space and time, which we've already introduced into our discourse. The other revolution was quantum mechanics, which revealed the intrinsic nature of reality, the threads that weave the world: a reality completely different from the one perceived by our senses, governed by surreal, counterintuitive laws that contradict and stand outside our lived experience.

Quantum mechanics is essentially a mathematical construction. Scientists contend that it constitutes a stupendous description of the functioning of everything and, although no one still knows quite why, it functions so well as to never have failed since it was first formulated. Satellite transmissions, the internet, computers, and nuclear medicine, all of which are practical applications of quantum physics, have radically changed our daily lives.

The staircase in the development of this discipline is engraved with the names of scientists of genius, such as Max Planck, Niels Bohr, Paul Dirac, Werner Heisenberg, Wolfgang Pauli, and others. At the base of quantum mechanics is the fundamental notion that all reality—matter—is made of tiny, discrete (separate), indivisible packets called *quanta*: a quantum is a measure that represents the smallest possible portion of any object. It was born from Max Planck's study of electromagnetism, when he imagined that the energy of an electric field was not transmitted in a unique flow, but in individual units of energy.

Planck long believed that his hypothesis was purely mathematical and not, in effect, a description of reality, but Albert Einstein realized and succeeded in demonstrating that those little grains were real, and that photons, the carriers of electromagnetic force, also have a corpuscular nature. Later, as Niels Bohr was studying the structure of the atom, he began to perceive that granularity characterized not only the *quanta* of light, but of all nature.

Bohr came to this certainty as he observed the movement of electrons around a nucleus and asked himself why the electrons didn't collpase into the nucleus. He decided that the phenomenon could be explained only by postulating that electrons can occupy only certain quite precise orbits around a nucleus (orbits where they can avoid irradiating or absorbing energy, which would lead to decay), and they shift from one safe orbit to another not by crossing through the space between them, but by jumping from one orbit to the next. Thus he had discovered the famous *quantum leaps*, that is, the shift in position of electrons as they orbit around the nucleus. Exactly what the expression *quantum leap* meant, and why an electron could follow only certain defined orbits, still remained entirely in the dark.

It was Werner Heisenberg who began to grasp the matter, and it's said that the intuition came to him as he was walking one night along a street illuminated by streetlamps, and noticed a man who came into view as he walked under one of the lamps, but disappeared when he passed into a dark zone.[45] Obviously, the man did not disappear, but only seemed to be visible or invisible according to whether his steps brought him into or out of the light. A man is a large, massive object, Heisenberg thought, but perhaps an electron could truly disappear, because it is much much smaller than an atom, and infinitely smaller than a man.

He then began to conjecture that the electron must appear, as it passes from one orbit to another, only when it interacts with something—in the case of the man, the interaction had been with the light of the lamppost—but has no precise position when it is not interacting with anything else; in which case it is truly nowhere.

The idea was mind-bending to say the least, but it was quickly followed by an even stranger one: that electrons exist only when they interact with something. In fact they materialize with a probability calculable with extreme precision, but it cannot be known with absolute certainty where and when such interaction might take place.

Heisenberg had realized that quantum leaps are the mode of being, or the mode of self-manifestation—the two are the same—of an electron. Soon this characteristic revealed itself to be a property of all sub-atomic particles.[46]

Heisenberg's hypothesis was formulated as the *uncertainty principle*, a cornerstone of quantum physics, which establishes the impossibility of knowing the position and velocity of particles at the same time, because the fact of measuring them (that is, the very fact of observing them) modifies their effectual state.

As is known, Einstein could not bring himself to accept the uncertainty principle, saying, so it's said, that he could not accept that God would play dice with the universe. Einstein's perplexity is quite understandable; it is indeed hard to imagine that reality, so complex, fragile, and improbable (as we have seen), emerges out of sheer chance. But quantum physics does not actually substitute Newton's vision of an ordered, predictable world with a chaotic mechanism governed by chance.

Rather, the uncertainty principle sanctions the end of the rigid determinism of classical physics in favor of a more open dynamic of the multiplicity of possibility, by virtue of which it is no longer acceptable to claim that the future is rigorously inscribed in the past.

As far as our own questions are concerned, what we have already begun to grasp and will discover with ever greater clarity moving forward is also true on the quantum level. Everything seems to be the result of a continuous interaction between chance and necessity, freedom and regularity, which always leaves space for the unexpected, for creativity, and for novelty.[47]

The entire mathematical scaffolding of quantum mechanics was finally completed and formalized by Paul Dirac, second only to Einstein in the Twentieth century as a genius of physics. Thanks to the equation that bears his name, we are today able to calculate with extreme exactitude the probability of locating an electron in one of its possible orbits.[48] In elaborating his equation, furthermore, Dirac also deducted the existence of anti-matter, an insight confirmed experimentally several years afterward.

A world most strange

No matter how strange the sub-atomic world may seem, it is the most real one, because it is exactly at that level that nature shows its most intrinsic nature, no matter the larger and larger combinations with which we experience it, from the microbe to the galaxy, from the cell to the human being. It's impossible to understand without letting go of all preconceived ideas about reality, nor can we trust the evidence of our senses. Great freedom of thought is required to read and interpret an ever more incredible world, and we need an equally free and potent imagination, as we learn from the tales of the scientists who have studied it, many of whom have won the Nobel Prize.[49]

The discovery of color offers an excellent example of the inadequacy of our senses for understanding the true nature of things. It had always been thought that color was a property of matter, although no one quite knew what type of property it might be. Only in the mid-Nineteenth century did Scottish physicist John Clerk Maxwell, who we mentioned previously, in discovering the wave motion of light, find out that color is the frequency of the electromagnetic waves that constitute light. High frequencies tend toward blue, while low frequencies tend toward red. Matter, therefore, must absorb light and emit it with a different frequency according to its composition; what we see as color is actually the light emitted by a vibration (a frequency) that our eyes translate into color because we are unable to see electromagnetic waves.[50]

Some characteristics of elementary particles are so strange as to make them seem more metaphysical than physical entities; for example, the fact that they can have a double nature, manifesting either as particles or waves;[51] or that they shift position without passing through the intermediate points between one position and the next; or that they penetrate solid bodies, as in the case of neutrinos who continuously pass through us by the billions, without our bodies registering any perception of it; or that they have no individuality, such that all particles of the same type are indistinguishable one from another no matter where they are; or that they do not age. This last is the case of photons, for whom time does not pass because they travel at the speed of light. Their time is eternity.

There is still more. If, in fact, the quantum nature of physical reality (matter and energy) and its properties may leave us shaken and amazed without radically impacting our philosophical approach to being, the fact that physical reality is also *relational* overturns our thought in ways well beyond the simple acceptance of evidence presented as scientific fact. An experiment conducted by physicists at the University of Geneva in 1977 revealed a characteristic of particles—perhaps the most incredible of all—called *entanglement*: the fact that two particles who have interacted by sharing the same wave function remain forever connected one to another, such that for any action performed on one of them, the other one reacts instantaneously, as though they were only one thing, no matter how far apart they are. As we've said, this fact demonstrates that all things stand in some way in relation to one another.[52]

Quantum physics thus induces us to reflect on a metaphysical plane concerning the nature of *something* that seems to pervade every aspect of life down to the ontological structure of being, revealing a world made of relations, interactions, clashes, and events. This is just what we saw happening in the first instants in the life of the Universe, when there existed only particles and quantum fields in continuous, fluctuating interaction. This was a world in formation, whose future was not—and is not—determined by necessity because, no matter how improbable that things might turn out differently, in both theory and practice they may. What happens happens *not because it cannot not* happen; rather, it is in the realization of one among many more or less probable possibilities that makes things turn out the way they do.[53]

The unpredictability of the behavior of a particle expresses a freedom in matter which, no matter how small, is nevertheless fundamental and true. In affirming the principle that any question, "any physical observation, to be precise, has an unpredictable, initially indeterminate response," quantum physics has shattered Newtonian determinism and introduced uncertainty into the world of physics. It may not be freedom in the full sense, but nevertheless "seems to open a chink in the wall."[54]

And that's enough for us.

Appendix to Chapter Two

Some further notes

Time.

Carlo Rovelli maintains that time is an illusion despite that fact that we perceive it as a real dimension and it clearly appears to run in a single direction. Why so? Rovelli explains it thus: "Physics and philosophers have come to the conclusion that the idea of a present time common throughout the universe is an illusion, and the 'universal flow' of time is a generalization that does not work. . . . But whether illusion or not, what explains the fact that, for us, time 'goes by', 'passes', 'flows'? . . . The way toward a response comes from the intimate link between time and heat, the fact that past and future are different only when there is a flow of heat, and the fact that heat is bound to physical probabilities, and that these in turn are bound to the fact that our interactions with the rest of the world do not distinguish the finest details of reality. The flow of time indeed emerges from physics, but not in terms of an exact description of the state of things. Rather, it emerges in terms of statistics and thermodynamics. . . For a hypothetical extremely acute vision that could see everything, there would be no time that 'flows' and the Universe would be a block of past, present, and future. But we conscious beings inhabit time because we see only a faded image of the world. . . Our perception of the passing of time comes from this blurred perception of the world . . ." Carlo Rovelli, *Sette brevi lezioni di fisica*, 65-68.

A single superforce?

"The physics of the last century led in the direction of a theory of the 'unification of forces'. We identify four fundamental forces in nature: gravity, electromagnetism, and the interactions, weak or strong, that act within atoms. But progress in theory (especially in a theory called supersymmetry) has led physicists to the idea that these four forces were once unified into a single force which emerged immediately after the Big Bang. Called superforce, it comes directly from the equations of physics extrapolated backwards in time. But what was this superforce, a single, immensely powerful force in nature, that governed our universe when it was extremely young? In truth it is something unknown and mysterious, and it is responsible for the fact that we are here." Amir D. Aczel, *Perché la scienza non nega Dio*, Milan, Raffaello Cortina Editore, 2015, 66.

Atom.

"Every atom is composed of three types of elementary particle: protons, endowed with a positive charge; electrons, with a negative charge; and neutrons, which have no charge. Protons and neutrons are crowded into the nucleus, while electrons spin around it. The number of protons is what grants the atom its chemical identity. . . It has been explained to me that while protons give the atom its identity, the electrons give it personality. Neutrons do not influence the identity of an atom but contribute to its mass. The number of neutrons is usually about the same as the number of protons, but may vary slightly either more or less. Adding or subtracting one or two neutrons, we obtain an isotope. . . The nucleus is extremely small, since it occupies [an infinitely small] part of the entire volume of an atom, but incredibly dense, containing almost all its mass [if the atom were a cathedral, the nucleus would be the size of a fly, but would be heavier than the cathedral] . . . The thought that atoms consist mostly of empty space—and that the solidity we experience all around us is illusory—is still a disturbing idea. In the real world, when two objects meet. . . they don't hit one another: 'Rather,' Timothy Ferris explains, 'negative fields. . . repel one another . . . If it were not for that charge, they too, like galaxies, could pass through one another unharmed.' When you are sitting in an easy chair, you are not really in contact with it; you levitate above it at the height of an angstrom (one hundred millionth of a centimeter), because your electrons and those of the easy chair firmly oppose any greater intimacy." Brayson, *Breve storia di quasi tutto*, 158-159.

3. Pikaia gracilens *and other matters*

Our search for indicators of freedom in action in the dynamics of the world now leads from the cosmos to biology. Is there some relation between biological life and freedom? Is it possible to hypothesize a freedom that manifests itself in organic life at the most basic level, well before we can speak of fully conscious life? If not, we would have to deduce that freedom is not an intrinsic property of reality, but concerns only *homo sapiens*. Freedom thus would be nothing more than free will, in which case we would conclude that it is produced by that mystery we refer to as consciousness, and thus, as some have claimed, an amazing but illusory product of the physics of the brain.

Just as a series of extremely precise cosmic conditions allowed for the formation of our planet, another equally extraordinary sequence of equally precise characteristics have resulted in an environment beautifully adapted to the formation of biological life. Someone (I no longer remember who) has even called the Earth *a gigantic incubator*. I'll summarize a few of the characteristics that in a certain sense represent the necessary *prerequisites* for the appearance of life.

First of all there's the moon: thanks to its size and vicinity, it exercises a stabilizing function on the Earth, keeping it turning obliquely on its axis. This has permitted and continues to permit the Sun to irradiate the Earth in a constant manner, thus providing the first "necessary condition for the evolution of life."[55]

The Earth has a nucleus composed of heavy metals (mostly iron and nickel) and is divided in two parts. The inner part is solid and temperatures are extremely high, almost as high as the surface of the Sun. The outer part is liquid. Around the nucleus is the so-called mantle consistently primarily of rock and around that lay diverse strata of the ever thinner material that forms the crust.

This arrangement has consequences absolutely fundamental for biological life. First of all—as is evident from the presence of volcanoes, hot water springs, and geysers—the core of the planet is hot, and the internal heat expands toward the surface. At the level of the mantle, heat derives from the decay of radioactive elements that generate, "a sort of current named the 'convection cell'," which is responsible for continental drift.

Volcanoes play an important role because through a complex geo-chemical cycle, the carbon dioxide they emit contributes to the so-called *natural greenhouse effect*, which maintains Earth's median temperatures that allow water to remain in a liquid state and form an atmosphere composed, until two and a half billion years ago, of water vapor, nitrogen, and carbon dioxide. But another key element is required in order to form organic molecules: free oxygen.

> The ultraviolet rays of solar radiation, unobstructed by the atmospheric ozone which had yet to be formed, directly struck the terrestrial surface, prohibiting the beginning of life. The rays did, however, manage to penetrate and be absorbed by the oceans, favoring the development in particular of blue-green algae. These algae were able to trigger a process of photosynthesis of chlorophyll, consuming carbon dioxide and producing oxygen. Little by little, this was how the atmosphere formed that we breathe today, which is currently 21% oxygen. The atmosphere, that is, has not always been the way it is now: the evolution of living things has profoundly modified the atmosphere over time. Also remember that—and this is no small detail—the Earth has a force of gravity sufficient to hold our atmosphere in place.[56]

For all these reasons and many others we won't pause to dwell on, the Earth developed into a perfect setting for biological life, which then came about. What determined this evolution? Once biological life began, what factors made it proceed in one direction rather than another? Was only one direction possible, with no eventuality that things might have taken a different path? In sum, are the mechanisms of the evolution of life determined by necessity, or do they leave space for freedom and alternative outcomes?

Organism and freedom

One of the first people to investigate the relations among life, matter, and freedom was German philosopher Hans Jonas, who is credited among other things with initiating the modern debate about bioethics. He held that there is such interdependency between freedom and living organisms that we can reasonably claim that where there is life, there is at least the germ of liberty and, vice versa, where there is a germ of liberty there is certainly organic life. This conviction runs like a red thread through Jonas's intellectual career, and is the fundamental thesis of his 1973 essay *Organismus und Freiheit*.[57]

Jonas argued that freedom was the essential distinctive characteristic of the living being and that this freedom must be manifest from the simplest forms of life, prokaryotic cells devoid of a nucleus. How so? Through the metabolism, which Jonas identified as the distinctive element of living as opposed to inert matter, and thus the substantive expression of the earliest form of freedom.[58]

In the still incomplete search for an unambiguous definition of *life*, Jonas held that one could speak of life wherever there was metabolic activity. He called his position an "'ontological' interpretation of biological phenomena", which allows us to take a philosophical approach toward biological reality that can finally restore its deserved primacy, which had been lost due to the Cartesian distinction between "the mental and the material".[59]

Jonas's extremely interesting idea is that freedom and life are grafted one into the other to such a degree that the presence of freedom is the differentiating element between an *organism* and a *thing*. He writes,

> We expect to encounter the concept [of freedom] in the realm of the spirit and will, but not before, and even if we do encounter it somewhere, we would expect to find it in the dimension of doing rather than in that of receiving. But. . . our thesis is that freedom can be distinguished even in metabolism, the base strata of all organic existence; metabolism, in fact, is the first form of freedom.[60]

From this perspective, life and freedom substantially coincide.[61] Let's examine this more closely. Both organic and inorganic matter are forms of matter, but they are so in different ways, and it is the distinction that defines them. The cell, organic matter, has the property of nourishing itself by assimilating matter external to itself, transforming that external matter into itself without itself mutating its own *form*. I eat an apple and it becomes part of me; something of that which I am made changes. I assimilate water, vitamins, fiber, minerals, but my own aspect does not change.

Inorganic matter, on the other hand, changes its own form in relation to that which is external to it, but it does not change its own *substance*, which is defined by an atomic number. Measuring the number of protons in its atom identifies it definitively: whatever form that particular inorganic matter takes on, its atomic number does not change. It remains invariable. In other words, no matter whether nugget, ingot, or necklace, gold is always gold.

Just the opposite happens with living organisms: no matter what they feed on, they conserve their own *form*—cell, bacterium, self—while the *substance* of which they're made changes: light, water, food. I eat a fish, a carrot, or a steak, and I change in a certain mode and measure the ingredients that keep my body alive, but my aspect remains the same. It is precisely this independence of form of living matter that for Jonas comprises the original, intrinsic freedom of the organism, the first *ontological quality* of the living being.

The cell that assimilates nutrition from outside distinguishes between itself and the external environment from which it draws nourishment. Wanting to live, it reaches beyond itself and has a purpose in doing so.[62] We can say that from the beginning, the organism takes an interest in itself; it recognizes what is useful and what is damaging to itself.[63] It chooses to take into itself other cells (or their parts) which keep it alive, but avoids those which could make it die. In sum, every single cell has a purpose concerning itself that gold certainly does not have.

This mechanism functions very well, a fact of which we are the best proof, with the billions of diverse cells we're made of, each of which performs its task extraordinarily well to keep us in good health.

Jonas's idea allows us to imagine a germ of freedom manifest already at the cellular level, although in an embryonic form adequate to its *simplicity*.

Even within the functions of metabolism, however, the same antinomy between liberty and necessity that we have previously encountered turns up once again, and will become ever more evident as organisms evolve in complexity to reach higher and higher levels of consciousness and intelligence. Freedom and necessity coexist in an organism, because while it is certainly separate from and independent of matter, and distinguishes and makes use of what is different from itself, it also is *obligated* to perform these actions in order to survive.[64] It is absolutely dependent on the very matter that it takes in and transforms. Thus it is free and dependent at the same time, a situation shared in common with every level and form of existence. The more conscious and strong the freedom, the more complex and articulated becomes its interactions with necessity.

In the biological world, like the realms of physics and metaphysics, the dialectical and ambiguous nature of freedom "rooted in the being of the organism as such" is manifested in the inevitable confrontation with necessity, seeking an equilibrium forever uncertain and unstable.[65] Necessity is bound to organic freedom like its shadow, a connection that returns enlarged "in each stage of its ascent to higher degrees of independence", "toward higher levels, in which freedom builds on freedom, the greater over the lesser, the more complex over the simpler."[66] This conviction compels the philosopher to consider human and divine freedom together, and to determine that they cannot be disentangled one from another.

Evolution: chance or necessity?

"Is starting from the properties of quarks and electrons to predict the existence of cows simply too complicated, or is it fundamentally impossible?"[67]

With this somewhat paradoxical question, physicist Peter Hoffmann sought to point out the impossibility of explaining the phenomenon of *life* through its component elements, and to indicate at the same time the unpredictability of the future. "Particle physics," he explained, "is indeed necessary to produce a cow. . . but obviously that's not enough." It isn't possible to predict the existence of a cow starting from what it's made of, because the future is neither rigidly predetermined nor predictable in detail. There is never only one possible future.

This is the next problem for us to take up. We are trying to understand whether the path that led from atoms to molecules, from molecules to cells, and step by step to ever more complex forms of life, is one determined by the power of necessity or not. What made things unfold in such a way as to achieve such an improbable and totally complex result as intelligent biological life?[68] Once all the ingredients were in place in this great laboratory of Earth, was it inevitable to arrive at humankind, or might we have never come about? Some maintain that once the elements necessary for biological life were assembled together in a suitable environment such as the Earth, nature over time would perform its alchemy and life was almost sure—or, some insist, absolutely sure—to appear, although it might likely have turned out quite different from the life we know. The famous paleontologist Stephen Jay Gould may have been the first to cite the cinematic metaphor of Frank Capra's *It's a Wonderful Life* (1946), later repeated by many of his colleagues, "Wind back the tape of life. . . let it play again from an identical starting point, and the chance becomes vanishingly small that anything like human intelligence would grace the replay."[69]

Gould uses the word *contingency* to encompass many unpredictable, accidental, and unrepeatable factors that come into play in the formation and becoming of life. On a superficial level the concept of *contingency* could seem similar to the *chance* that one of the founding fathers of molecular biology, 1965 Nobel Prize for Medicine winner Jacques Monod, identified as the definitive formative principle of the origin and evolution of life.[70]

The role of random chance in evolution is unquestionable. Still, the fact that genetic mutations are random does not mean that chance is the only factor by which life evolves; such an idea leads to an erroneous conception of nature and evolution.[71] Genetic mutation is the fruit of an error in the replication of DNA, and thus certainly determined by chance, but such is not the case of natural selection, which favors individuals who carry an *advantageous mutation* and tends to eliminate disadvantageous or damaging mutations. Error therefore has an intriguing role. The fact that the incredible, sophisticated variety of creatures are born from error—an accumulation of errors—alongside devastating diseases and genetic syndromes can help us better understand the connections that underlay every aspect of reality. In a certain sense nature seems to progress in a way similar to the development of each human being, as though both processes were guided by the same principle: error, mistakes, and imperfection are necessary to life and wellbeing. They are part of the process of growth. If nature had never made mistakes, the Earth might have been populated by nothing but bacteria, by simple, perfect prokaryotic cells.

It actually seems to be the case that perfection, like absolute symmetry, is sterile and unproductive, and that things happen only when there is a *space for maneuver* which works out diverse solutions by trial and error. Action, movement, and change happen only when there are alternative possibilities. A kind of openness, the necessary premise for a multiplicity of consequences, is therefore freedom itself.

Once again we encounter the ambiguity—the simultaneous presence of choice and necessity, good and bad outcomes of the same active principle—that appears to be a litmus test of freedom. Ambiguity is a symptom of which freedom is the cause.

At the opposite pole of the hypothesis that randomness dominates evolution we find a viewpoint based on absolute determinism, which considers life, what presents itself before our eyes, as the predictable and inevitable product of the chemical and physical laws of evolution. Such a view conflicts with a great deal of observational data that refutes its claims.

Archeological evidence reveals that the evolutionary history of life on Earth has not followed a linear path, from simple origins toward ever greater specialization and complexity, without risk or alternative outcomes. On the contrary, scholars agree that life has developed in leaps and bounds: long periods of stasis followed by sudden change and evolutionary acceleration. Phases of prosperity and consolidation have been brusquely interrupted by the near-total destruction of living things.

Many strokes of luck have brought us to where we are today. The most famous of these was the huge meteorite that hit 65 million years ago, the main cause of the extinction of the dinosaurs. As a result, a small rodent (our ancestor) seized the unexpected opportunity to emerge from its underground den, spread across the planet, and evolve, instead of remaining the easiest available food for the great carnivores.

Another history tells us about many other fortuitous breaks in the predictable plotline of life, which took place long, long before the dinosaurs, but thanks to which we have come to be as we are. One such is the story of *Pikaia gracilens*, its discovery and what it revealed. It's a tale worth telling.

The first hero

Pikaia gracilens is the first great hero of the future history of humanity and is, like all true heroes, mild and modest. We know of *Pikaia* thanks to Charles Doolittle Walcott (1850-1927), the famous American geologist and paleontologist who found her fossil by chance (as often happens, or is said to happen) in 1909 near Burgess, a town in the state of British Columbia in the Canadian Rockies. *Pikaia* turned up in a fossil deposit which would turn out to be the richest and most important such deposit of the Cambrian Period, circa 500 million years ago.

Having found it near Mount Pik or Pika, he named the fossil *Pikaia*, adding *gracilens* in honor of its graceful form. He described it as,

> ribbon-shaped and segmented, flattened laterally, between three and five centimeters in length, with a rudimentary head, two antenna-like protuberances, a wider, flatter posterior with which it fluctuated in the water, very similar to the modern amphioxus (or lancet-fish, a small marine pre-vertebrate chordate).[72]

Walcott, however, did not realize exactly what he'd found, and classified the creature among the polychaete worms in the phylum of the annelids.[73] Upon Walcott's death, research in the Burgess fossil field (called the Burgess Shale) passed on to Harry Whittington, a paleontologist expert in arthropod-trilobites, the ancestors of insects, arachnids, and crustaceans. He identified two animals called Marella and Yohoia that belonged to no known phylum and did not seem to be simple precursors of later, more complex and evolved species (at the time, evolution was thought of as a continuous progress from simpler to more specialized forms). As far as Whittington could tell, Marella and Yohoia were ideally adapted to live in their Cambrian environment.

To delve more deeply into the matter, Whittington assigned graduate the-
ses on these fossils to two students, Simon Conway Morris and Derek Briggs,
who devoted the years 1976 and 1977 to re-examining in greater detail all Walcott's findings. They discovered that *Pikaia* was not in fact an annelid, because
it had a rigid dorsal column containing bands of muscles in a zig-zag pattern, in
what was clearly an ancestral form of vertebral column. Thus *Pikaia* must have
been a chordate, a creature belonging to the same phylum as human beings. It
was the earliest chordate ever found, perhaps the first to have existed.

What Morris and Briggs' studies brought to light above all was the entirely new fact that the Burgess animals were not primitive and simple, but already
highly specialized. Walcott's idea that the Burgess Shale was a sort of collection of samples of organisms that could be tracked to modern descendants was
wrong. It became possible to imagine a different history of evolution, in which,
"instead of having a narrow initial base that constantly expanded over time,
multicellular life reaches its maximum variety at the beginning, while later decimation allows only certain anatomical plans to survive."[74]

Among the Burgess Shale fauna it is possible to identify 25 different basic *architectures* (anatomical plans), only four of which ever evolved into the
groups of highly successful species still present and dominant on Earth today.
The survivors were neither more numerous nor better adapted nor more efficient
than the ones who didn't survive.[75] In reference to the organisms of the Cambrian Period, we might adopt the remark Telmo Pievani made about Neanderthals,
which he took from Jack Nicholson in the film *Prizzi's Honor*: if they were so
damned adapted, why are they so extinct?

An abundant organism in the Burgess Shale were the *priapulida*, the first
important soft-bodied carnivores, whose typical form we can guess from their
priapic name(they belonged to the phylum of worms). The polychaetes belonged
to the same phylum but were much more rare. And yet today, the former have
become extremely rare, while the latter have prospered and spread virtually everywhere. "Obviously," Gould comments ironically, "something dramatic (and
disastrous) has happened to priapulids since the Burgess."[76]

The unexpected dramatic event that took place, not only for *priapulida*
but for all the Cambrian animals who lived in the Burgess Shale, was very probably the sudden collapse of the sheer limestone cliff, derived from millennia of
deposits of algae, at the base of which they lived, in a muddy bottom-land rich
in air and light. Their extraordinary conservation is most likely due to the fact
that the abrupt collapse of the overarching cliff killed them and buried them in

mud, an environment devoid of oxygen and the *scavenger organisms* that would consume their remains. Few major disturbances took place afterward.

As we've said, thanks to the Burgess Shale the early Cambrian is considered the era of greatest experimentation and flexibility in the development of body shapes. The primeval explosion of life forms was followed in the late Cambrian by the great decimation. Little *Pikaia* survived, however, despite her slim chances. She was a prey organism,

> but for us being a prey turned out well, due to a conspiracy of concomitant processes in which selection interacts with other change factors and the accidents of setting. A Cambrian bookie would not have placed much of a bet on the chances of this little animal. Through *Pikaia*. . . we have an alternative counter-future, who knows whether more or less probable, in which the human presence among the vertebrates might have been inconceivable, to the advantage of the possessors of exoskeletons such as the trilobites and other "terrible shrimp".[77]

If Pikaia had not survived, it is almost certain that *Homo sapiens* would never have appeared. We exist thanks to her, an escapee from the decimation at Burgess.[78]

The Cambrian tragedy provides evidence that the flow of events is not irreversibly inscribed. And yet it is also not merely random. We are children of an unpredictable concatenation of events fortuitous for us, and of circumstances, roads taken and not taken, which we can comprehend and reconstruct only posthumously. Biological life has evolved from the beginning not without order or meaning, but also not in the only way possible. We've gotten here, but we also might not have: we are "the product of a massive historical contingency, and if we started the film of life over from the beginning a thousand times, we would probably never have come to be."[79]

Contingency

The story of *Pikaia* introduces the topic of contingency and its role in the history of life, which Gould describes this way:

> If a remote event shifts, even in the slightest degree and in a way seemingly devoid of importance, evolution will enter a radically different channel. This. . . possibility represents nothing less than the essence of the story. Its name is contingency, and contingency is a thing in itself, not an attenuation of determinism through the operation of chance.[80]

In this way, contingency introduces a third element that stands between rigidly deterministic causality and the absence of causality (the total randomness of events).

What is—what do we mean by—contingency? The word derives from the Latin verb *contingere*, to happen. In philosophical terms, contingency is the property of beings that can either be or not be; that is, it expresses a concept opposite to that of necessity. In common language, it is also a synonym for circumstance or possibility. However it is used, it always indicates something that takes place but might just as easily not have taken place. Like chance it is not predictable, but it is different from chance because, after having taken place, a contingent result may be interpreted and understood through the diverse causal factors that determined its outcome. Telmo Pievani explains this clearly:

> If on a decidedly unlucky day a man takes his dog out for a walk and passes under a gutter in the exact moment a big roof tile falls, we say that it was an "accidental" death. What happened? The causal chain that led the man to go out with his dog precisely at that time and take precisely that route (and before that, his having bought a dog despite living in a condominium, and having moved to that city, and so on) intersects ironically with another causal chain, in which poor maintenance leads to the deterioration of an old roof, and from this to a roof tile breaking off and sliding down during a rainy, snowy day, and finally to the gust of wind that triggers the tile's vertical flight that ends at exactly that point on the sidewalk in that moment.[81]

Each event within the single causal chain has its indubitable logic and the whole sequence can be reconstructed comprehensibly. Chance and determinism intersect through contingency, in the sense described by Charles Darwin to Asa Gray as "laws in the background and contingency in the particulars."[82] What makes an event random is the intersection of chains of cause and effect that lead to a given event, even though the two chains "are completely independent one from another. They are autonomous and their conjunction is merely possible."[83] When something happens that might not have happened, but which we can reconstruct *a posteriori* in a logical sequence of cause and effect, we are dealing with a contingency. Applied to our appearance and evolution on Earth, this means that we are here, we are what we are, but we also may not have been, or we may have been completely different. Still it is equally true that life is an implicit possibility since the Universe was nothing but a hydrogen cloud and the tiniest variation in its parameters would have been enough to deprive us of the opportunity to be here, talking about it. Considerations of this type have originated an idea known as the *anthropic principle*, which we will discuss in the next chapter.

Right now we are facing the beginning of the long walk of humanity, a path far from linear, certain, or predetermined, and made "of rules similar to laws, repeated patterns of evolutionary dynamics", lucky breaks and unpredictable misfortunes, inflexible natural law and surprising singularities.[84] Gould concludes that

> We are the offspring of history, and must establish our own paths in this most diverse and interesting of conceivable universes . . . offering us the greatest freedom to thrive, or to fail, in our own chosen way.[85]

Evolution: the luck of being here

Everyone knows that living organisms evolve through a process that combines different factors, such as random genetic mutation and natural selection, that favor the chances for reproduction of individual carriers of mutations favorable for survival. Through this mechanism, positive mutations spread and consolidate, becoming part of the genetic patrimony of descendants. Even if the best does not always survive, the trait most adapted to the given environment tends to carry on, even though the environment may change unexpectedly, reshuffling the cards as in the example of *Pikaia gracilens*. The road that leads from our shrimpy ancestor to ourselves has been tortuous, complex, and often deviated by improbable, beneficial twists. With evolutionary development, the emergence of the genus *homo,* and then our own species *sapiens*, lucky breaks, circumstances, and coincidences have accompanied with increasing impact the effects— sometimes fortunate, sometimes catastrophic—of human freedom.

In order to track the footsteps in that path and reconstruct the general outlines of the sequence, we have to consider vast swaths of time that, compared to a human life, seem like eternity.

The planet Earth was formed 4.5/4.8 billion years ago. The first billion years allowed for cooling, the formation of a solid crust, and the development of a habitat favorable to organic life, which appeared around 3.8 billion years ago in the form of single-celled prokaryotes whose fossils have been found in the Earth's most ancient sedimentary rock (in Greenland). It appears that the prokaryotes—bacteria, blue-green algae, and stromatolites—dominated the planet for about 2.5 billion years, reproducing by self-division, always equal to themselves, until for some unknown reason something interrupted the placid symmetry of things and more complex cells called eukaryotes appeared, featuring specialized organelles and a central nucleus containing genetic matter. Fossils of this type date to circa 1.4 billion years ago. These cells (to whose domain we humans also belong) also reproduced by self-division. After this innovation came a new period of stasis, and for hundreds of millions of years the Earth was populated by monocellular organisms. Approximately 700 million years ago the bland tranquility of everyday life was once again shattered by an anomaly: a eukaryote cell divided but instead of separating from the *mother*—probably due to a copying error in the transmission of its genetic patrimony—the *daughter* remained attached. This was the chance discovery of collaboration, a winning innovation that generated the first multicellular organism.[86] This was our true beginning.

We are standing at the threshold, so to speak, and things start moving faster and faster. After *only* 100 million years, toward the end of the Precambrian Era (preceding the Cambrian, the era of *Pikaia gracilens*) "the oceans begin to teem with more complex beings. . . [and at] 570 million years [ago], the enigmatic fauna of the Ediacara makes its entrance, composed of the bizarre multicellular beings found in southern Australia on the Ediacara Hills of the Flinders Ranges."[87] The fauna of Ediacara seem to have been organic life's first great attempt to expand its potentialities, a sort of natural experiment with no durable outcome, demonstrating "that life experimented with separate strategies, repeatedly 'trying out' [new forms]."[88]

During the Cambrian period, multicellular life manifests itself with unequalled richness and variety. After an early phase of miniscule capsule- and bowl-shaped organisms, very complex and anatomically varied fauna begins to appear.[89] After billions of years of cellular life, "no fewer than three distinct types of fauna emerge, each of which unleashes a vast diversity of forms."[90] We are now facing the so-called Cambrian enigma, an explosion of life and forms that Darwin himself was the first to call a true mystery and recognize as a possible refutation of his theories.[91]

In truth, the Cambrian findings do not undermine the overall theory of evolution, but only the idea that it took place in a linear way, from simpler organisms to successively more sophisticated forms, following a fixed and definite trajectory. Nor do the Cambrian fossils raise doubts about natural selection, but rather about the assumption that it always favors the creatures most adapted to their environment. On the contrary, the record shows that environments change, and what survives are the less specialized organisms which are more capable of adapting to environmental mutation. In sum, the most important thing is that the documentation sends us a signal not "of gradual change, but of general stability with sudden bursts of change."[92] Species tend to remain stable in equilibrium amidst surrounding innovation, "without actual gradual change in a particular direction. Only occasionally does the equilibrium break, the stasis is interrupted, and a new species suddenly appears on the scale of geological time."[93]

Despite that fact that over the course of evolutionary history we have often been a whisper away from no longer existing, and we repeatedly stood on the brink of extinction even before becoming human, scholars such as Gould, Pievani, Manzi and many others do not think we are the result of a toss of the dice. Rather, we are the outcome "of a permanent historical contingency."[94] They are convinced that "there was nothing ineluctable in our history. Rather, it is the fruit of circumstances. Not of random chance, be sure, but of circumstances."[95]

Survivors

Let's return to circa 600 million years ago when, as we said, change began to accelerate. To understand how fast, we can borrow from the Six-day Creation story in the Bible. If the Earth, as Genesis says, was created at midnight on Sunday, then the first bacterial cells would have appeared on Tuesday morning around 8:00 a.m. The microcosm would have evolved over the next couple of days, achieving completion on Thursday at midnight. At about 4:00 p.m. on Friday, microorganisms would have invented sexual reproduction (the most favorable means of transmitting genetic material). All the forms of life would have evolved on the Sixth Day. The great apes would come on the scene at 11:40 p.m. on Saturday night and the first forms of *homo sapiens* would arrive thirty seconds before midnight. *Homo neandertaliensis*, our older cousin, would dominate Europe between 15 and 4 seconds before midnight. We would have arrived in Africa and Asia 11 seconds before midnight, and come to Europe 5 seconds before the bell. Finally, "recorded human history begins circa two thirds of a second before midnight."[96]

In that last day, life would have repeatedly risked extinction, passing through numerous *bottlenecks* that each time left Earth with a terrifyingly small number of living survivors. Experts speak of six mass extinctions: three in the Paleozoic (only the first of which our *Pikaia* would have survived); two during the Mesozoic (the first, nearly 250 million years ago, wiped out 96 percent of living things, both plants and animals); the last during the Cenozoic (the era we are living in today) approximately 65 million years ago. This was the extinction that killed off the dinosaurs and from which emerged the little rodent ancestor of all mammals, including ourselves. This event seems to have influenced the planetary climate for the next 10,000 years. Without the gigantic providential meteorite that caused the Cenozoic catastrophe, today we would probably be, according to the most optimistic calculations, a hardy species of mole.

But here we are instead, *homo sapiens*, the most invasive, intelligent, successful, and dangerous species on the planet. What do we know about ourselves?

In sum, we know this: We belong to the *family* of *hominids*, whose evolution began around five million years ago, more or less two million years after the passing of the last common ancestor between us and the great humanoid apes.[97] Thanks to information culled from the analysis of mitochondrial DNA on a global scale, we know beyond doubt that we originated in Africa and descended from a rather small number of individuals; not exactly Adam and Eve, perhaps, but no more than a few thousand individuals.[98] The study of Y chromosomes has also fully confirmed both the African origin and the singularity of the human species. We know for certain that anyone who insists on subdividing humanity into different races cannot claim anything in nature as an alibi.[99] The only possible answer to the question of human races is the one given by Albert Einstein to a clerk who asked him his race for a passport application: the human race. All other differences are environmental and cultural.

Paleontology has provided us with convincing data that the evolution of the genus *Homo* has taken place in jumps and starts which were provoked, guided, or favored by climatic mutations. Radical changes in habitat upset the anatomical stability of our progenitors. We are still quite a young species, but we've enjoyed extraordinary success due to factors which do not always do us honor: we are extremely aggressive, dangerous, and hegemonic, but also very smart (not all of us, however). We have probably contributed (not always with violence, it must be said) to the extinction of other species in our same genus who once shared the planet with us. Circa 150,000 years ago, when the Earth was undergoing a turbulent period of climate change, there were at least four species of *Homo*, subdivided roughly so: *sapiens* in Africa, *neanderthal* in Europe and western Asia, *denisova* in north Asia and Siberia, and *floresiensis* in southeast Asia. In the end, we are the only ones standing. *Sapiens*, in any case, is different from the other types of *Homo* that preceded and shared its path. Not merely "an improved version on our ancestors," we are "an entirely new entity":

> a new conception, qualitatively distinct in important although limited ways. Even if our egoistic species tends to overestimate the degree of qualitative difference between itself and the rest of the living world, including our closest relatives, the difference is real. The extraordinary phenomenon that we represent must be understood, if possible, in terms of its utter uniqueness.[100]

The search for what it is that renders us unique is the matter of infinite studies and discussions in both scientific and philosophical settings. Although unanimity is still quite a ways off—and difficult to reach, given the subjectivity involved in interpreting phenomena—it is nevertheless a widely shared view that a special prerogative we enjoy is awareness of ourselves and the surrounding world and the difference between the two. We know we are part of the world, but we also know how to distinguish between ourselves and the world. We can set ourselves off from it and are able to manipulate it, think about it, and interpret it. No other animal does that quite the way we do, and the current state of the science suggests that the other members of the genus *Homo* were not able to do it at the same level as *sapiens*.[101]

Nevertheless, we still do not know when nor how we acquired this capacity. Some scholars maintain that it must have come about suddenly and all at once; others on the contrary see it as the fruit of a long, gradual process. Fossils show decisively that there are no anatomical differences, but only cultural and historical ones, between ourselves and the first *sapiens* of 200,000 years ago. The most ancient likely sign of symbolic activity is an incised ochre slab incised with regular markings found south of Cape Town, South Africa, in the Bomblos Cave, datable to 75,000 years ago. We will probably find more artifacts as study continues, but for now the material evidence becomes truly extraordinary around 35,000 years ago, the era of the incredible and famous cave decorations in Chauvet, Lescaux, Altamira, and similar sites. There, unknown artists left incontestable signs of artistic sensibility and skill, revealing a clear perception of their individuality.[102]

These paintings convey the indefinable aura of an intuition of worldly transcendence and of a consciousness both worldly and spiritual. After all, why would someone want to leave traces of their lives if they had no idea of a time beyond their own, and, in a sense, of the value of their existence in relation to some greater whole of which they are a part? Does any other animal do this?

All these peculiar human abilities lead back to the much-studied but still mysterious phenomenon we call consciousness. To reduce it to the most essential terms, the inquiry into consciousness tries first of all to understand what it is, why and how it formed in human beings, and whether it is a purely physical phenomenon or if there is something else involved.

The only point of deep disagreement between Charles Darwin and Alfred Russel Wallace, the two men who simultaneously and independently developed the theory of evolution by natural selection, concerned their views of the origin of human consciousness.[103] Darwin claimed that consciousness emerged as a consequence of the evolution of the brain through natural selection, just like everything else in the biological world. Wallace, on the other hand, saw things differently. Ian Tattersall tells the story of their dispute:

> Wallace, however, was unable to understand how natural selection could fill the gap between human cognition and that of all the other forms of life. On the contrary, the breadth and depth of the discontinuity between symbolic and non-symbolic cognition was obvious to him, and he recognized that the first could not simply be an extension of the second. Blocked by his inability to involve natural selection, Wallace ended up attributing the origin of the modern intellect to a supernatural agent. Because of this interpretation, Wallace is still an object of mockery—but in reality his fundamental intuition is quite acute. Wallace had clearly understood that natural selection is not a creative force that generates new, more desirable structures for pleasure. On the contrary, the law of natural selection works solely on what already exists. From a biological point of view, function must necessarily follow form. Innovations must present themselves spontaneously and in this sense must always emerge not as *adaptations*—characteristics adapted to a particular style of life—but as *exaptations*—new characteristics not connected to present circumstances, but which can potentially be used in new ways.[104]

As to the nature of consciousness, the first scholar to elaborate an overall conception of the mind based on the idea of a totally biological and evolutionary root was biochemist and neuroscientist Gerald Edelman, who won the Nobel Prize for Medicine in 1972 (shared with his colleague Rodney Porter). Edelman made a distinction between two forms of consciousness: a primary form, possessed by some superior animals, is the ability to integrate observed events with memory to create an awareness of the present, the immediate past, and the surrounding world. The second form of consciousness is of a higher order and is characteristic only of human beings, entailing the elaboration and expression of feelings and the capacity for abstract thought. For Edelman, one represents the evolution of the other in such a way that the second, more evolved form doesn't substitute new abilities for the old ones, but adds new skills while conserving the earlier ones. He stresses in particular that the added abilities include a sense of oneself encompassing the past and future which can be synthesized as "the consciousness of having consciousness".[105]

The connection between mental activity (whose instrument is the brain) and consciousness is clear. In a certain sense we can consider consciousness to be a non-physical product of the activity of a corporeal organ; neuronal activity translated into an interpretation of lived experience. The task of consciousness may be to provide a sense of meaning to cerebral activity, because the brain performs many tasks unconsciously, leaving the mind to provide a meaning *a posteriori* (Michael Gazzaniga). As regards "awareness of one's mental state" (Joseph LeDoux), consciousness is the awareness of self, knowing that one is alive, and the ability to recount experiences and emotions.

We speak about ourselves to ourselves and others in the form of a narration *post facto*, filtering events through our own personal interpretation. Events come out of this process enriched with the meanings we give them, demonstrating our capacity to elaborate experience cognitively. We do this with words, our species' most important evolutionary innovation, perhaps, after the invention of standing erect. Words grant us the power to remember, learn, teach, and build up both experience and awareness. This is what makes our species unique and probably stronger than all other animals. Scientific studies have confirmed that all living beings have *something* similar to consciousness, a quality that grows ever more sophisticated as one ascends the evolutionary scale from bacteria to primates to *sapiens*. Still, we tend to think of ourselves as the only beings fully conscious of the outside world, our own individuality, and the relation between the two.

Most of all, we are the only beings who ask themselves questions about the meaning of life and whether we are alone in the Universe, what death is, and why we die. Useless questions, perhaps even damaging from the point of view of survival, and yet unequivocally human.

The human mind is different from that of the other animals, even those whose brains resemble our own, because it is able to elaborate abstract thought, using devices such as symbols and complex, immaterial ideas. The human brain produces thoughts and visions of the world. It is incapable of limiting itself to merely observing what exists; it interprets, formulates, and manifests its particular interiority by granting meanings to things that transcend their physical boundaries. Although not the only species to produce magnificent things, the human is an artist. Spiders weave webs so beautiful and astonishing as to seem works of art, but they do so driven by instinct and patterned instructions they have borne inside for hundreds of millions of years. From the spider's point of view, the web is solely a perfect trap for capturing prey. The spider has no larger intention.[106]

We have already alluded to the fact that *sapiens* is a reality different from all the other members of its own genus. Its appearance on the scene signals the beginning of *history*. Before being inscribed on stone or papyrus, its history is first evidenced in graves and the remains of encampments; in skeletons and bone fragments; in stone objects such as arrowheads. Before moving on, let's say a bit more about this creature.

Sapiens appeared circa 200,000 years ago as an animal with new and unique characteristics. It emigrated from Africa in successive waves, probably in a continuous flow of small groups of individuals, and began to populate Europe, intermixing with a resident population of the same genus but a different species named *Neanderthal* (after the Neander Valley in Germany, near Dusseldorf, where their remains were first uncovered).[107]

The first European *sapiens* are called Cro-Magnon, after the cave in the Dordogne region of France where its first skeletons were found. The Cro-Magnon lived together with the Neanderthals, who we know buried their dead and looked after the weakest members of the group, practices that demonstrate they were "complex beings who had particular, sophisticated ways of interacting with and perceiving the surrounding world."[108] In an effort to explain certain behaviors which turn up sporadically and suggest a level of conceptualization and symbolic capacity similar to that of *sapiens*, scientists have hypothesized that the Neanderthal may have adopted Cro-Magnon conduct and techniques such as ordered burial plots and associated rituals, signs of nascent forms of religious life and supernatural beliefs.[109]

Although many pieces of the puzzle of the evolutionary history of our species are still lacking, available information confirms a process that was neither continuous nor gradual; no reassuring linear ascent from less to more evolved forms. It is no longer possible to represent human development the way schoolbooks once did, with a series of anthropomorphic primates walking ever more erect until the triumphant transformation into a spear-wielding *sapiens*. As far as we know today, we can represent evolution like a giant tree of many branches that reach outward, interweave, and often end suddenly, as though cut off. Millions of years of speciation, cohabitation, and extinction have led to a picture of "many ways of being human up to a handful of millennia ago. . . It has been a race among many athletes up to a couple of meters before the end, and none of the runners was the same as the others."[110]

This race might have ended in a myriad of ways: with us alone as victors or with our extinction, in any moment, for any motive. Nothing was inscribed from the beginning.

Let that stand as a rapid summary of the long, complex path leading from the simplest unicellular organism to the emergence of a conscious being capable of imagining the workings of the Universe and life. A being capable of building tools to prove its imaginings not mere wondering but intelligent comprehension of reality, in a world whose nature far surpasses any imagination. We now leave *Homo sapiens* to its history, fruit of all the elements we have turned up thus far—chance, laws of nature, contingency—plus a final factor indispensable to mankind's quest for fulfillment and freedom. That factor is the ability to determine the outcome of events by consciously choosing among diverse alternatives. After *sapiens*, freedom becomes free will, although we have still a long way to go before we understand what that means.

Appendix to Chapter Three

A Confirmation and Many Uncertainties

The freedom of the cell.

Hans Jonas would have been pleased to learn the results of a discovery that validates his philosophical conception of the organism. The finding concerns the role performed by the plasmatic membrane—the thin surface of a cell—which transfers matter, energy, and information from outside to inside. In performing its task, the cell demonstrates discernment, since it selects what to admit and what to ignore; an act that can be configured as an expression of its own freedom. It is "precisely in this correlation between organism and freedom—which is such that wherever there is an organism, there is at least the germ of freedom—that we can identify the most original aspect of *Organism and Freedom*." (Paolo Becchi, "Introduzione" to *Organismo e libertà*, XIX).

The cell exercises discernment like so: "Through proteins that act as receptors and passageway, the membrane selects out what interests it from what doesn't, what it absorbs and what it excludes. Each cell is an intersection of a wide range of atoms, molecules, and other organisms that fluctuate around it. Each time the cell creates a contact it exercises a moment of primordial discernment. . . . [The cell normally remains enclosed and sealed], but when it encounters molecules that possess a certain particular configuration. . . it responds in an entirely different way. The molecules of its own membrane attach themselves to this new molecule. The cell then alters the structure of its own membrane so that this molecule can be admitted. Thanks to such discernment the new molecule becomes part of the internal environment of the cell, which in this way finds and captures its "food", the energy molecules it assimilates. The action of discernment is fundamental. Mistaken choices can lead to death. . . . At the boundaries of its own body, therefore, each cell makes certain elementary choices: Is this a risk worth running? Is this other entity a source of nourishment? Will it increase my chances of staying alive?" (B. Swimme, M. E. Tucker, *Il viaggio dell'universo*, 56.)

Evolutionism.

The theory of evolution is shared by the majority of scientists on the basis of scientific evidence and the data assembled thus far. Nevertheless, it is still rejected by some fundamentalist groups in the United States who, based on a literal interpretation of religious texts, propose an alternative hypothesis called Creationism which they consider equally sustainable from a scientific viewpoint. In so doing, rather than raising doubts about science, they perform a poor service to religion. The issue has little relation to the questions pursued in this book, so we have chosen not to stir up that particular hornet's nest. Here we consider evolution to have been amply demonstrated as true, and we are convinced by Darwin's theory of evolution through natural selection and random mutation. We consider this theory in no way incompatible with religious faith, especially as regards Christianity derived from the Bible. This does not imply that there may not be different opinions concerning interpretation of details of this or that specific aspect of evolution. Even such disagreements, however, manifest universal agreement concerning evolution as an interpretive framework.

The origin of life: random or necessary? The origin of life remains one of the great unsolved mysteries along with the origin of the Universe and of human consciousness. The most common opinion is that life originated from inanimate matter through successive "chemical states that determined a spontaneous and continuous increase in complexity and molecular functionality," (Fritjof Capra, Pier Luigi Luisi, *Vita e natura. Una visione sistemica*, 277), leading to the emergence of proto-cells able to reproduce themselves identically by assimilating elements from the surrounding environment. This is a phenomenon that even many scientists disinclined (if not openly hostile) to religious conceptions do not hesitate to describe as so improbable as to seem miraculous. (Edoardo Boncinelli, *Prodigi quotidiani*, 80) We are still in the dark as to the succession of chemical events and the triggering factor that produced such a result. It has not been possible so far to reproduce the sequence in a laboratory. The question is whether the effect was produced by pure and simple randomness, or through an inevitable succession of events. Certainly ". . .mutations are random, as are genetic exchanges, but taken all together, evolution clearly does not proceed in a random manner. Nature is highly sophisticated in its selection of efficacious mutations. In order to be 'accepted', a mutation must respect numerous conditions and restrictions. Over all stands the principle of structural determinism, which means the acceptance only of changes coherent with the deep structure of the living organism and its organization. Furthermore, the mutation must produce a minimal alteration that respects the principle function of the living cell, which is self-maintenance. The individuality characteristic of the cell must be preserved. . . . Still further, the mutation must permit some adjustments to environmental changes; last of all, it must conform to the laws of physics and chemistry that govern cellular metabolism. . . . This presupposes the non-linear dynamics of a network of chemical reactions that permit only a limited number of new forms or functions. All this is quite different from Monod's position of 'only by chance'". (V. Capra, P.L. Luisi, Vita e natura, 275)

The origin of consciousness.

We still do not know what brought us to this peculiar phenomenon we call consciousness. Darwin's idea, in disagreement with his colleague Wallace, was that consciousness emerged like everything else, from evolution. For Ian Tattersall, on the other hand, "its acquisition was an emergent event probably of little impact in terms of physical or genetic innovation, relatively sudden, that appeared quite late in our evolutionary history," without leaving physical traces in bones or teeth. (Ian Tattersall, *Il cammino dell'uomo*, 208-209). Tattersall hypothesizes that our cognitive skills emerged "from a convergence of unrelated characteristics", a mutation something like the feathers of birds, which served functionally to protect them from the cold and only later came to be co-opted for the purpose of flight. Another similar example is that of human fingers, which allow us to play the piano but did not evolve for that purpose. "At the moment of the appearance of *Homo sapiens*," writes Tattersall, "the evolution of the human brain must have already taken place, for whatever reason, to the point that a small genetic change. . . was sufficient to produce a structure endowed with a completely new potential." (Ian Tattersall, *Il mondo prima della storia*, 135). A valid objection comes, however, from Telmo Pievani, who observes, "Claiming that the evolution of consciousness was an inevitable process, and basing this claim on the concept of adaptive convergence, is however in clear contradiction to the fact that over three and a half billion years of the history of life, human consciousness as such evolved one time only! In a huge span of time that corresponds with almost half the possible duration of the Earth itself, the experiment of human consciousness remains, in the absence of contrary evidence, unique. And all this stands in contradiction of the fact that on many occasions a hair's breadth kept it from not evolving at all." (Telmo Pievani, *La vita inaspettata*, 134). The mystery remains and does not seem close to being solved.

4. *The origin of evil*

Being and nothingness

The preceding chapter concluded with the coming of *Homo sapiens* and its peculiar form of liberty expressed in the ability to decide how to think and act on the basis of personal considerations, inclinations, and preferences. This is what is commonly termed free will, which we think of as permitting us to distinguish between good and bad, and allows us to perform good or bad actions according to our will. Whether or not our will is always free or on the contrary always conditioned by diverse factors is still an open question after centuries of debate, and we will not pause to dwell on it here. Instead, the object of our reflections will be a more radical question, which precedes the ethical and moral implications of free will, and which serves in a sense as its basis. This is the question about the origin of evil itself.[111]

We shall return to our initial inquiry: *why is there being instead of non-being?* We have postulated that being came about as the expression of a will capable of willing itself, without being rooted in something outside itself, and without any other motivation than its own will to exist.[112] We have called this will capable of self-realization *God*, a word-compendium of concepts of origin, abyss, and transcendence.

The next step is to ask ourselves who this *God* might be. Even if we know that any answer can be only partial and to some degree subjective, it remains an inevitable and fundamental question. What can be said of God? First of all, we must recognize that God is *not being*, since God precedes being and autonomously determines that it should exist.[113] Secondly, we must acknowledge that God is the origin of reality (this is what we mean by saying that God *created the world*). God is the only entity that exists solely because God so wishes, and is exactly what he wishes to be. God is determined neither by nature nor by any necessity, but only by his own freedom. Given this basis, we have concluded that

God is above all absolute, unlimited liberty. This does not mean that freedom is God, but rather freedom belongs intrinsically and originally to God, his first and most fundamental attribute.

In the vision we are delineating here, God does not resemble the necessary entity imagined by some philosophers, but rather the biblical God, who is presented as *he who is* by his own choice and wish (as we will see in more detail in Chapter Six). He who could *not be*, or to say it more clearly, who would have been able *not to exist* (*non esser-ci*), in the sense that he could have decided to remain within himself without ever having set the cosmic dance in motion (*esser-ci*: Pareyson's translation of Heidegger's *Dasein*, the word *esser-ci* combines the infinitive *essere—to be*—with the adverb of place *ci*, used to mean something potentially encompassing both *there* and *here*; in a sense, *present*). In such a case, we existent entities would never exist, neither as ourselves nor as anything else, not even in the anguishing possibility of nothingness.

This is a fundamental passage. The freedom that expresses itself with maximum power in the divine will to exist is the same freedom that has made possible, in the same moment, its negative alternative, nothingness. Before the divine decision to exist (*esser-ci*), there was no nothingness. The same impulse from which existence arose rendered nothingness a real possibility but a path not taken. The unique origin of being and non being is the sign of a primeval ambiguity that has penetrated and continues to permeate reality, from the beginning and forever, in its every aspect. This ambiguity is like a shadow cast on God himself, making God also ambivalent; a dispenser of evil as well as good, the originator both of life and death.[114]

In this sense divinity is double-edged—*ancipital* is Pareyson's term—meaning it is what the ancients spoke of in many myths and which finds its emblem in the two-faced Roman god, Janus.

Eternity and history

We now enter into a truly nebulous and fascinating zone of Pareyson's vision, imagining a time preceding the emergence of God from himself. From our point of view, the beginning coincides with creation, with the initiation of existence as we know it; a unique event, something like what science calls a *singularity*, an uncaused event from which everything else springs.[115] This is the moment when God, so to speak, decides to exist. The *ci* in the term *esser-ci* comprises, or expresses, all that is not God, and for which he is God. From the viewpoint of God as well, emerging from himself is an *event*, a choice, an act of freedom that expresses a dynamic internal to himself. A change takes place in divine life from one condition—being within himself—to another one: emerging from himself. Any time there is an event, there is necessarily a story that can be told as such. Thus we can speak of the *history of God*, a story that unfolds in a time that is not ours, a time that does not yet exist. There is no *before*. Before there is only "God before God": God who has not yet chosen to emerge from his solitary perfection to make way for the world.[116] That is the time of God, a time that is other, different, eternal, infinite, unknown, and yet real and true because something took place in it. And since there is an indissoluble logical nexus between action, freedom, and history, we can speak of a divine history that precedes any other history.

Divine actions, such as the choice to be and the rejection of nothingness, are *events* that tell the story of God, which cannot be put into words except in the form of a myth intended to unveil the true nature of reality, of which reality conserves the imprint:

> Because of his eternity it might seem impossible to tell the story or narrate a myth of God. But it is possible, because God is freedom, and his acts, like all free acts, give rise to historical events. Where there is liberty, there are events, and where there are events, there is history. In fact, where there is freedom there is history, and where there is history there is liberty. If God is freedom, there is a history in and of eternity, which could not be if God were a necessary being, or a being for whom freedom were a property rather than an essence. . . No matter how eternal, this history never ceases being history, and its events can never become dialectical moments. Far from being a one-way dialectic on an obligatory path, with necessary steps and an inevitable outcome, the history of God cannot not be narrated like a story filled with unexpected, unpredictable events. The history of God is like an intensely revelatory myth able to touch the center of reality, because its object is freedom, and freedom is the heart of the real, the meaning of things.[117]

The dialectic mentioned in this citation has nothing to do with the Hegelian dynamic of thesis, antithesis, and synthesis. Instead, it expresses the experience available to all of the encounter/clash of opposites—life/death, good/evil, necessity/freedom, joy/pain, and so on. From this clash the space opens up in which events and freely-decided actions take place, which are nothing less than the unfolding of history.[118]

Divine history is also marked by the "clash of opposites", because of which we can speak of history outside of the world and human time, in the dimension that precedes the beginning. God had to fight against something in order to come to exist; not against nothingness, but against a *temptation* intrinsic to himself, the dialectical opposite of his will to exist: the temptation not to exist. In choosing to exist, to be present, he rejected nothingness and simultaneously instituted being as a good, as affirmation, as a choice of positivity. Saying God exists means saying that the good was chosen.

> God is not the good, but the will for the good: absolute positive freedom, positivity affirmed as the victory of good over evil, the definitive overcoming of annihilating negativity. God is not the good, but the chosen good, good freely chosen over evil; good willed in the presence of the possibility of evil, good emerging victorious from the originary alternative.[119]

Reviewing the considerations made concerning God up to this point, we have said that: 1) we can speak of God philosophically only if we avoid any demonstrative intention; 2) saying *God* essentially means saying there is an origin, a cause, a motive, a meaning, a why; 3) any discourse on God is an interpretation of the experience of the divine on the part of the speaker; 4) God is neither a necessary nor a necessitating being; on the contrary, God is absolutely free, the source of all liberty. God is good not out of necessity, but by choice; the good chosen definitively.

But if this is so, then where does evil come from?

The B side

Evil has two faces. The first, in which it manifests its ontological origin, is *evil in itself*. The second demonstrates the effects of evil in action, the abstract potential translated into the concrete reality of suffering inflicted and undergone. We call this second face *active evil*; it is the most serious proof of the existence of *evil in itself*. The question is what transforms *evil in itself* into *active evil*, into suffering?

Thinking about *evil in itself* requires reflection of a logical-metaphysical nature. Thinking about the effects of evil, about the actuality of pain, we must find an explanation that permits us to believe that existence is not merely a cruel, senseless joke. We need an explanation that demonstrates that good exists and is possible notwithstanding the real power of evil.

Pareyson held that philosophy had long demonstrated itself inadequate to the task of facing this problem, that it had been unable to offer fully satisfying answers, neither in terms of logic, nor in respect to experience. This subject has been increasingly marginalized by philosophy and left instead to poetry, myth, and forms of narrative, which have dealt with the issue quite forcefully. Greek tragedy, for example, has spurred philosophers such as Salvatore Natoli to a vast, profound reflection on pain.[120] The novels of Dostoevsky justify thinking of him as a philosopher who reasons about evil and suffering by means of narration. The biblical Book of Job stands as an extraordinary meditation on the silence of God in the face of unjust suffering.

Within the realm of philosophy, however, there still needs to be a reflection on evil that combines logic, experience, and interpretation.[121] The presence of evil seems to negate the existence of God. Suffering, especially that of innocents, confirms God's absence, because it's obvious—so it's said—that God would never permit such a thing. But such reasoning is "desolately simplistic. Atheism as a consequence of the recognition of evil is the fruit of theodicy, a misunderstanding that derives from God's goodness the idea of its negation as simple privation."[122] But evil is much more than this.

What is it, then? What is evil from an ontological viewpoint? Above all, where does it come from, and what originates it?

The metaphysical origin of evil

Reality originates in an absolute, primeval freedom we can call *will*—an evocative, fitting noun—or God, a word that we've said summarizes in one verbal entity the concepts of the abyssal, of potency, and the incommensurability of an initiating principle. There where everything began we must seek the origin of evil; that is, in God himself, because otherwise we would collapse into Manicheism. On the other hand, if there is some original nexus between divinity and evil, then moral evil—that which is present historically in our world—cannot be explained solely "on the merely ethical plane, but requires an ontological explanation."[123]

If in the maladroit effort to absolve God of all responsibility we prefer to conceive a God untouched by evil, completely ignorant of evil, then we would have to consider good and evil as equally powerful principles, or as two separate divinities of good and evil in combat one against the another. Or we would have to entertain a fundamentally inconsistent vision of evil simply as the absence of good.

In a philosophy of freedom, none of the above hypotheses holds water: the negative is not privation, but the *affirmation* of negativity, a real, rock-hard opposition, "impetus toward destruction and instinct for death, which with terrible efficacy and sinister vigor infiltrates and cleaves the entire world."[124] This negativity is the other possible form of being, rejected but impossible to eliminate. "Thus the classical alternative no longer makes sense: either theodicy, which cancels out evil, or atheism, which cancels out God. The actual choice is either to cancel out both God and evil, or affirm both God and evil."[125]

There is a shadow in God, and not looking at it serves neither to conceal it or cancel it out:

> In the heart of reality there is not only positivity but also negativity; and between these two terms . . . there is . . . tension and struggle. The power that animates both good and evil is freedom, but precisely because of that, freedom is disassociated, double-edged, ambiguous . . . capable of affirming itself in the very act of negating itself, a negative impulse that is at the same time the power of self-destruction and total destruction . . . The ambiguity of liberty that animates the Universe has repercussions on everything because it somehow introduces negation into everything, even into divinity. Reality, which humankind faces as much with horror as with wonder, is ambiguous. Mankind is ambiguous because it cannot achieve goodness without also causing evil; only through pain can it achieve joy. Divinity is ambiguous because it is the God of anger and of grace, of glory and agony, at the same time. The majesty of omnipotence cannot be unaccompanied by anguishing, terrible self-destruction.[126]

This is an unquestionably strong statement which can shock and disturb. Aware of the temerity of his discourse on the "evil in God", Pareyson seeks to attenuate his audacity by recalling Christian mystics such as Meister Eckhart (who declared that *God is nothingness*) and Angelo Silesio (who still more radically claimed that *God is pure nullity, a black and authentic nullity*), and by specifying that the claim must be understood in its mythic quality and its philosophical, rather than moral, significance. Still, it has a powerful impact and calls for clarification.

First of all and most importantly it means that evil can only be explained on an ontological, originary level. Second, it points out an ambiguity inherent in divinity itself. Lastly, by positing the origin of evil in God while also insisting that God is not the author of evil, the claim liberates God from the concept of causality: God does not provoke evil, nor is the cause of evil to be found in God. Not being *cause*, God is not the foundation, and is thus restored to his true essence, which is that of being *origin*, "liberty and abyss, which is to say something much more than a foundation."[127] Pareyson concludes,

> This conception of the presence of evil in God does not reject a conception of divinity as positivity, because it insists that God is not the author of evil, and rather than doing evil God contains it and contains it in the form of possibility. On the other hand, it avoids the ambiguous definition of God as good, which is inadequate to his level, inconsistent with his transcendence, and incapable of explaining the sheer abundance of evil in the history of human beings, where it has produced the most horrific, terrifying devastation.[128]

Let's consider the ontological aspect of evil. Evil is not part of divine nature; neither does it pre-exist God. Evil is made potentially possible by being because it represents being's opposite, nothingness, which threatens being only from the moment of its inception.[129] From the primeval decision by which God gave life to himself and reality, nothingness arose as well, but it arose already defeated by the choice made in favor of existence. In eternity, from the beginning and forever, real evil is the discarded possibility, rendered inactive by the choice of life and the good.

So where does the trace of ambiguity in God come from? From the fact that amidst all these developments God came into contact with negativity, even if only in the act of conquering and rejecting it. In experiencing this, however, God was somehow touched by negativity, and conserves it like a shadow. Because of this, we must admit that evil is present in God, howsoever "as a defeated, overcome possibility."[130]

From the point of view of being, therefore, evil is its negation, or rather its nullification, and it sprang from the originary freedom in the very moment of the free choice to exist.

If this were not so, if there had been no alternative to being, there would never have been freedom and life would be an ineluctable effect of the nature of the world. The question as to where evil comes from would have no answer outside of ourselves and our history. Evil would have come into existence alongside human beings and their free will. If on the other hand not necessity but freedom stands as the origin of all, then evil must be present, at least potentially, since the beginning as the negation of positivity, long before humankind came along to render it *active*. Good and evil are put into motion by the same energy, freedom, but the positive—the good—has priority, because it was the chosen alternative. The origin of evil is metaphysical and not to be found in mankind. Man is merely the guilty party, the one who is capable out of sheer wickedness of transforming evil from an abstract possibility into a concrete act. If humankind did not exist, evil would exist just the same, but there would be no one to commit acts of evil. Man and God differ in this with respect to evil: God, who could have chosen evil (*non-being*), instead chose the good (life) and did so once and for all, while mankind chooses evil when it could instead choose good.

In this clash between will, freedom, and various choices, a gap was created between divine life and human life, a gap in which the humus of evil produced the seeds of divine, human, and cosmic pain and suffering. In the eternity of divine time evil has been discarded, but in the time of mortality in which humans are immersed, evil works through us. God must bear this evil and stems it. This is the enigma of suffering that unites God and mankind in a bond, or rather in the shared experience that Christianity interprets through the mysteries of divine incarnation and human redemption. Thanks to the irrevocable divine decision in favor of life, humanity is bestowed with eschatological hope.

At this point we can understand why the discourse about evil cannot be solely ethical and moral; rather, it is "a religious discourse *per excellence*," a spiritual discourse that can neither remain silent in the fact of suffering nor refuse to grant evil its meaning. It cannot abandon the hope that good *ultimately* prevails.

The reasoning developed here on the nature of evil undoubtedly derives from how one interprets reality, but this fact in no way renders it less compelling or convincing. What about the *truth*? This we cannot know, since truth can only be found "within the single interpretation one gives of it."[131] Mankind, in fact, can approach the truth—which can never be reduced to a single, definitive formulation—only through individual experience, which is necessarily partial and subjective. That is to say in other words that a truth probably exists, but we can never possess it, only hypothesize it as we interpret the world.

The historical dimension of evil

When we pass from the metaphysical dimension to our own, the historical dimension, evil manifests itself in its violent, terrible reality. Where does such force come from if God has defeated it eternally?

An immense *cosmotheandric* tragedy takes place on the giant stage of the world in which the human and the divine clash, originating a reality in which existent evil cannot be neutralized or rendered inactive. Two protagonists face one another: on one hand absolute and positive freedom, on the other a less-powerful but equally absolute freedom which does not always choose the good. How can these two forces coexist? Primeval liberty and human liberty can be considered separately, but freedom is qualitatively whole and indivisible, "although marked by possible cesuras and leaps".[132]

One such leap certainly takes place in the passage from the metaphysical dimension to the human one. In a certain sense we can say that when freedom comes into play in humankind, the spiritual character of freedom acquires a physical dimension that manifests itself in the human capacity to translate potential evil into effectual action. The negativity rendered inert by God becomes actualized in the human dimension of time and space. This is what Pareyson means when he says *the origin of evil is in God but he is by no means its author.* God could manifest evil, but does not; we have the power not to, but we do. We are the wretches who actualize a possibility eternally discarded by God.[133]

By rendering nothingness vanquished by God as an active force that inheres in the heart of reality, human freedom demonstrates its power, which is great but not unlimited, as seen in the fact that being born and dying do not depend on us.[134] The situation and circumstances in which we come into the world, the succession of personal and historical events that mark each life, represent real factors that condition the freedom of each individual. Family, the historical circumstances one's lifetime, and gender are all factors that radically affect the effectual quality of an individual's freedom and they are independent of one's choices or desires. For many, such conditioning factors are enough to reveal that human freedom is an illusion. From a larger perspective, however, the situation *given* rather than chosen entails limitations, but it is at the same time the only condition in which it is possible to actualize freedom. Obviously one may come into the world by inserting oneself into a pre-existent reality which is independent of us, but only by entering that reality—by being born—can we be free, and it is certain that from the moment of our arrival, that same reality shall be changed by our arrival.

This means that the human being enjoys no liberty unconditioned by necessity or other limiting factors. Still, finding ourselves in a given specific situation does not impede the dynamism of individual liberty. Even in a situation with no way out, one is still free to choose one's attitude of response to that limit.

Every situation can be taken as *imprisonment*, or *fate*, or as an opportunity for self-realization. There is always a margin of choice even when the only choice is to decide what sense to ascribe to what is happening. For example, I could decide to give to someone the life that they want to take away from me; thus I would preserve a tiny but crucial crumb of freedom.[135]

The greatness in our freedom is that it permits us to transmute the ineluctable into a choice: being killed into giving life. The person who can transform sacrifice into a gift proves that freedom is inalienable because there is no subjection (passivity) that cannot be read as acceptance (activity).[136] To overcome the contradiction between necessity and liberty without negating the reality and interaction of both we must consider everything in light of Pareyson's dialectic of *gift* and *consent, giving* and *accepting* (or refusing). In this light it is possible to think of divine and human liberty together while preserving each one's own truth and absoluteness. It is in fact permissible and natural to ask ourselves "if mankind receives freedom—and cannot refuse it—does not this configure, from a human perspective, as a form of constriction? If we imagine humanity receiving something which it cannot *not* receive but which it is free to decide how to use, is not this a real, potent, and forceful liberty, notwithstanding the limits imposed by nature?

If we regard the encounter between divine and human liberty as a movement of gift and consent (that is, the voluntary welcoming and use of the gift, as seen in Chapter One), then the meeting becomes a relationship between two wills, each of which exercises its own freedom. Freedom is *given* to humankind like a substance that belongs to life, but it is the individual who *realizes* it (as a producer of the real) by the very fact of accepting it. In this sense man is always free, whether in acceptance and exercise of one's freedom or in refusal. Acceptance and rejection are both exercises of freedom. Although we cannot choose which deck to play with, we can decide how to play the cards or refuse to play altogether. By reading the opposition between liberty and necessity in this manner, we make it possible to include in our vision of things the concepts of gratuitousness, generosity, and love implicit in the common root of the words liberty and liberality.

What a strange thing the world is, said Jean d'Ormesson. In the face of such complexity, strangeness, and wonder, he observed that ultimately "the heart of the problem is knowing—or rather imagining, flipping the coin, deciding almost blindly—whether every life is absurd or whether the world has a meaning."[137]

And that's exactly the point.

Appendix to Chapter 4

Good and evil: a single abyss

The negative in God.

Pareyson maintains that the discourse on evil cannot be conducted satisfactorily on the ethical plain alone, nor can it be reduced to a question of guilt deriving from an infraction of moral law and thus bound to individual responsibility: "As concerns the beginning, if one considers only the passage of entities from non-being to being, as in ontic metaphysics, or the derivation of being from non-being understood as thought. . . as in classical idealism, that past of non-being contained in the beginning, once overcome, would have no relevance at all, and could never transmute into an active nullity. But what happens at the beginning is an irruption, or rather an explosion, of freedom, and freedom has such potent and efficacious vigor as to transform the inert negativity of non-being into the dynamic, robust negativity of active nullity, that is, of evil as an alternative possibility to freedom's affirmation . . . In a philosophy of freedom . . . nothingness is not peripheral, like a limiting border, or superficial like a decreed privation, but is central and profound, an inseparable companion of being, sharing its abyssal nature. . ." (L. Pareyson, *Ontologia della libertà*, 259-260). The possibility of nothingness is the negativity that would have been possible to achieve but was discarded and repudiated by the originary positivity. Such a possibility remains as a simple, faded trace of something undergone and overcome. This and only this is what Pareyson means by the evil in God. While certainly quite strong, the concept is not blasphemous; in the Bible itself (see Chapter Six), God repeatedly declares that it is he who makes evil and good, the one who decides life and death. If the choice had been different, if God had so to speak "extinguished" in himself the will to be, there would not be an evil god; rather, there would be neither God nor reality.

Theodicy.

The question of divine justice in relation to evil has found a place in philosophy thanks to existentialism and the centrality attributed to human feeling in relation to the world. Theology too has continued to take an interest in the problem, most specifically in the branch of theodicy, due to its commitment to refute the insistence that it is impossible to reconcile the hypothesis of an omnipotent, comprehensible divine goodness with the evident presence of evil in the world. On this topic Pareyson holds that "God, having made humankind as free as himself, has devoted himself to a destiny of suffering," because he does not exercise his power in coercion, but in persuasion. In its absolute respect for human liberty, divinity "while offering the good is ready to receive evil in return. It is not that God 'allows' evil; rather he actually suffers it." (L. Pareyson, *Essere Libertà Ambiguità*, 142-143).

5. *The problem of interpretation*

The vindication of metaphysics

Metaphorically driven away from the door of philosophy, the metaphysics behind this book have re-entered through the window of science, vindicated in the face of those who—in their understandable enthusiasm for ever more amazing scientific discoveries—had relegated it among the useless disciplines, charged with asking questions to which there can be no answer. Those who condemned metaphysics imagined that all possible answers could be provided by science.

Metaphysics is a discipline occupied with abstract problems whose solutions cannot be univocal, and whose proofs cannot be demonstrated by the unambiguous rules of scientific experimentation. It seemed that the scientific disciplines would have deprived metaphysics of interest and reason to exist. But as often happens, things have not turned out quite as expected. Rather than bringing to an end any speculation about the origins of existence—the so-called *ultimate questions*—science has brought them into the foreground, rendering them still more audacious and abyssal, precisely as a result of its ever more world-shaking discoveries.

From a philosophical viewpoint, cosmological interrogation into the origin of the Universe or the presence of meaning (if not purpose) in the cosmos is the most tantalizing science, while the natural sciences, especially chemistry and evolutionary biology, seem to touch the deepest, most sensitive chords of the human search for itself and its origins. From there, however, shifting the discourse into questions of who we are and where we come from—whether we are animals only slightly more evolved than others or, rather, something more than that—causes an abrupt change in climate. Where fair play rules in discussions of the cosmos and its laws, the dialogue now grows heated. The tone can become sarcastic and insulting. Contrary opinions are represented as belonging to a *nar-*

row minority, while one's own viewpoint is held to be that of *serious experts*. Since personal convictions, faith, and belief—matters irrelevant to discussions of the physics of the Universe—come into play, the acrimony among scholars is disturbing and annoying, making it hard for non-experts to distinguish reason from opinion.

The problem comes from the fact that, once a reality is recognized, it is normal to seek to interpret it within a comprehensive framework that goes beyond merely describing the components of that reality; to hypothesize, applying reason, a larger, global sense of it all. It is—or should be—clear that since interpretation is by definition subjective, it is also always open, incomplete, subject to doubt, and changeable. Interpreting the world through its phenomena, we are *seeking* rather than *describing* truth in the world. Thus the question arises: does a *truth* exist that encompasses everything?[138]

The ancients were certain of such a truth, and expressed their convictions in their cosmogonies and myths, passing them down orally from generation to generation before they learned to transcribe them in written form, perhaps abandoning oral memory. Inquiry later continued in philosophy and the sciences, which led to unprecedented knowledge of the true nature of reality. Paradoxically, by discovering so much, we have come to face how little we know; our ignorance grows together with our knowledge.

Today we are more cautious, more realistic, and less ingenuously triumphant with regard to reality. Although by definition necessarily a single thing, reality remains largely inaccessible to us, at least in terms of comprehending it as a whole. Luigi Pareyson was right in pointing out that we can only hypothesize reality within the interpretations we variously impose on it.

Nevertheless, although the portion of truth we succeed in bringing to light is only partial and provisional, this does not mean that it is arbitrary and purely subjective. Every interpretation must be founded on fact, on observed data and objective reasoning, and must conform to the requirements of rationality, which excludes the arbitrary and reins in subjectivity. The objective of research is to find an interpretive key for the existence of the world which our reason can accept.

Interpretation is never neutral. Its beginning, the spark that brings to flame the thinker's imagination (whether that thinker is philosopher or scientist) is an intuition. But once it is elaborated, the interpretation of the world expresses itself in action: in behaviors, attitudes, values; in an ethics, in sum, that in turn is only possible if the actions are free, and thus responsible. No action is fully responsible if carried out under coercion. In fact, judicial systems evaluate responsibility according to the degree of constriction to which a person is subjected. The primary connection is not between ethics and religion, because *good* and *just* conduct in reference to oneself, others, and nature, does not depend on religion, but on the freedom that permits discernment, choice, alternatives, and decision.

It is because of this that I am unsatisfied by conceptions of the world that negate or exclude freedom, in comparison to other conceptions that include freedom within an equally rational framework. Between rationally founded positions that admit or exclude freedom, I find more convincing those that include freedom. In this chapter I'll explain why.

Interpreting the Universe

Although we know a great deal, there are still questions about the Universe we have been able neither to solve nor forget. These are the scientific problems with metaphysical overtones we just mentioned, which are modern versions of the *ultimate questions* that have impassioned philosophers and theologians for centuries. What did the Universe come from? What makes its genesis, structure, and governing laws comprehensible to us? Perhaps the most intriguing and disturbing question of all is, what made something as complex and exceptional as intelligent life come about, and how? As seen in Chapter Two, the physics of the Universe are structured according to laws that are not only clear but, according to scientists, surprisingly simple, and thus absolutely intelligible. Next to those, however, are the laws of quantum physics that govern the same material of which the cosmos is made. These laws, although shown to be quite exact, are different from the basic laws of physics in being entirely incomprehensible. The realm of the infinitely small, the components of all matter, is both unpredictable and certain. The law of necessity that dominates in the larger dimensional world gives way to improbability and the indeterminate. The result is an ordered Universe on the macroscopic level, but one not *necessarily* predetermined, because the matter it is composed of is unpredictable in its behavior. As physicist Guido Tonelli has often observed, it is precarious, as we are, because nothing can guarantee that the Higgs boson, after serving for thirteen billion years (the age of the Universe) as the glue that holds particles—and thus matter—together, will continue to do so.

An unpredictable future excludes determinism and represents a foundational *prerequisite* of freedom. In the "many intrinsic unpredictabilities [that exist] in the processes of the physical world," British physicist and theologian John Polkinghorne perceives the creative freedom of the Universe. He terms this *freedom of process*, a "flexibility in the open process of the Universe," which represents the form of freedom inherent to the physical cosmos.[139] Making an analogy with free will, the human form of freedom, Polkinghorne proposes extending that concept to the natural world, recognizing *freedom of process* as its most intrinsic attribute. Like a person, the cosmos too has the opportunity to be itself. He explains,

> The Universe may not seem to be an organism, and still less does it resemble a machine. Fruit of the collapse of predictability is a freedom of development that makes physics able to accept not only the idea of being (that is, the eternal regularity of physical laws), but also that of becoming (the history, in continuous evolution, of complex systems). The future is not necessarily contained in the present.[140]

A comprehensible Universe

The greatest mystery in the Universe, which Albert Einstein didn't hesitate to describe as a true miracle, is its comprehensibility.

The Universe is governed by laws that the human mind is able to understand well enough to explicate its structure and dynamics through mathematics, a universal language shared by all. There is a consonance between the cosmos and mathematics manifest in the congruence between the human mind and the Universe, a congruence to which scientists give diverse explanations. Some hold that the world is intrinsically mathematical and that mathematics therefore must in some way precede the world. Mathematics therefore must have its own ontological status, as though it were the metaphysical substrate of everything. Others think that the human mind has a natural tendency to systematize the world, and that mathematics are simply an organizing instrument invented by humans to "impose a meaning and structure on the world."[141] Still others maintain that the rationality of the world is reflected in the mind's rationality, so that we comprehend the Universe because *we* are part of it. Yet others claim that we humans are the *consciousness* of the Universe; that is we are the Universe's *awareness of itself*, and thus we are capable of comprehending it.

We have entered the field of opinion and conjecture, and each position has its part of scientific dignity, as demonstrated by the total divergence between one Nobel Prize winner, Christian de Duve, and another, Jacques Monod. Monod envisions a Universe born by chance, sterile and indifferent to humankind, while de Duve imagines a Universe *fertile and gravid with life*:

> An entity endowed with meaning, made so as to generate life and the mind, destined to originate thinking beings capable of discerning the truth and apprehending beauty, able to feel love, desire the good, define evil, and taste mystery.[142]

The second great mystery that envelops the Universe is the fact of its being extraordinarily favorable to life.

We know that any minimal variation in the numerical parameters that regulate the constants of nature would be enough to impede life as we know it. Life is possible only because its perfect calibration since the beginning has produced exactly the physics and chemistry indispensable for life.[143] This complex phenomenon has been summarized in the statement that, "the essential characteristics of our Universe appear *finely tuned*; that is, accurately 'synchronized' or accurately 'regulated' for the appearance of life."[144]

The idea that the presence of intelligent life is the outcome of an accurate synchronization of the Universe has led to the formulation of the *anthropic principle*, an enigmatic concept that has resulted in quite a bit of misunderstanding and ideologically-motivated misuse.[145] An interdisciplinary argument has proliferated around this principle which has become so harsh as to violate the rules of courtesy and respect for diversity of opinion typical of scientific collegiality. The most interesting and philosophically fruitful aspects of the problem have been relegated to the background. The subject therefore calls for some clarification, beginning on a semantic level.

The anthropic principle

To begin with, a distinction must be made between *fine tuning* and the *anthropic principle*. The first is an objective datum derived from observation; the second is a hermeneutic theory, a philosophical interpretation of the metaphysical import of scientific data. The *anthropic principle* is not and cannot be considered a scientific theory, but only a significant hypothesis on a philosophical and theological plane.

In the second place, we need to better understand what the *anthropic principle* is, as formulated by Brandon Carter in two types, one called *weak*, the other *strong*. According to the *weak formulation*, the principle claims in substance that our presence poses precise limitations on the Universe and its evolution, and that any theory of the cosmos must take account of this factor. It is a matter of ascertaining something that our existence makes us certain of: we are here because the setting in which we find ourselves must have all the characteristics that permit our presence.

This version of the anthropic principle is irrelevant from a philosophical viewpoint: it takes account of a given fact and simply states that the conditions of the Universe and the coincidences that have occurred during its evolution were necessary to the appearance of life.

One of the most important scholars of this subject matter, Italian astronomer and theologian Giuseppe Tanzella-Nitti, has stressed that it may be misleading to call this weak formulation a "principle", because "it signals instead a series of facts which do not depend on the assumption of a particular philosophical perspective (just as the charge of electrons or the mass of protons does not depend on a particular philosophy), and in place of being categorized as a principle, we suggest it may be more correct to present it as 'biotic conditions'."[146] In this version, the anthropic principle offers no answer to the much more demanding philosophical question as to whether those conditions and coincidences were also *sufficient* to originate life. Due to its ideological neutrality and because it recognizes a purely objective datum, the *weak version* of the anthropic principle arouses no particular contestation in scientific circles. It is a basic, axiomatic statement that adds nothing to the evidence.

In its much more controversial *strong* formulation, the anthropic principle does not limit itself to testifying to the objective datum of the necessary compatibility between our life and the parameters of the Universe. Going beyond that, it asserts that all the conditions *necessary* for the evolution of life were also *sufficient* to make it evolve. In other words, in this version, life in general and the human being in particular are understood as predictable, inevitable results of the evolution of the cosmos. Given the premises, the appearance of life could not *not* have taken place in the forms in which we know it. Obviously, the strong anthropic principle has no scientific foundation, but it does bear important philosophical consequences, both because it inclines toward absolute determinism, and because it reintroduces the concept of a purpose in nature.[147]

To orient ourselves in this minefield, we turn to the studies by Tanzella-Nitti.[148] He begins by listing the things we can be relatively certain of, which are:

a) there is a strong interdependence between the history of the Universe and biological and human life;
b) the anthropic conditions favorable to the development of life are present from the very beginning of the Universe;
c) the Universe has evolved in a powerfully unified way.

The observation of these given facts, the scholar maintains, may lead us to comprehend the concept of purpose in three different ways. First, the acknowledgement of the numerical regularity encountered in nature that manifests an intrinsic coherence and order within nature itself, which could not be produced randomly. Second, the concept of purpose can be regarded functionally: evidence suggests that to create life there must be coordination between the laws of physics, biology, and chemistry. Third, we can interpret purpose in the strongest sense as implying the presence of an intelligent intentionality.

Numerical regularity and functional purpose, Tanzella-Nitti continues, concern science. Purpose as willed, intelligent intention belongs to the field of philosophy. These are two different orders of knowledge, the first consequence of which is that scientific claims can neither affirm nor refute the claims of philosophy, the only field which can provide space for ideas such as an intentional project, an intelligent mind (whether or not the cosmos is transcendent), or a Creator. Obviously, the opposite is also true, because philosophical claims about ultimate purposes cannot negate the claims of science.

In other words, Tanzella-Nitti intends to unambiguously affirm that scientific claims concerning the anthropic principle can be shifted or changed only by further scientific discoveries that may negate the numerical constants and the biological, chemical, and physical processes that led to life. The principle cannot be negated, on the other hand, by *a priori* statements or philosophical observations disconnected from empirical observation.

Vice versa, science lacks the instruments to negate purely speculative considerations about the objective data supplied by science. In their research into the foundations of the world, philosophy and theology cannot ignore scientific discoveries, and dialogue with science without assimilating themselves into it, because they respond to a different order of questions and are based on different statutes.

A final important observation must be made: in its weak formulation, the anthropic principle does not necessarily entail theism, particularly not in the sense in which it is generally intended by the traditional monotheistic religions.

Nor can the weak formulation demonstrate the existence of a design or purpose in nature that leads inevitably to life. Rather, it limits itself to demonstrating the coherence of and correlations in the structure of the cosmos.[149]

Fine-tuning

We shall now take up again the matter of *fine-tuning* and the question underlying it: how to explain the fact that the Universe is so favorable to the emergence of intelligent life? On the basis of what is currently known, there are three possible logical answers, each of which is authoritatively sustained by scientists—physicists and astronomers—and by philosophers.[150]

The first hypothesis supposes that our Universe is the only one in existence and that all the laws and conditions that determine it are, in turn, regulated by a universal super-law. This law sees to it that the Universe is the way it is and cannot be any different from what it is. This is a purely speculative hypothesis without empirical foundation, which can neither be negated nor demonstrated by rigorous logic. Still, it cannot be excluded that proofs in favor of this hypothesis may one day come to light.

The second hypothesis considers our Universe as part of a *multiverse* composed of an infinite series of universes: it must be that we live in the only one in which, by sheer chance, conditions adapted to the emergence of life have come into existence. Critiquing this hypothesis, biochemist Christian de Duve maintained that if our Universe were one of a myriad of possible universes, it would be, "the random product, equal to all the other universes, of an accidental fluctuation within something described as 'chaotic void'."[151] In this hypothesis, the fundamental role would be played by chance, but we have already said how and why chance is an unsatisfactory and virtually unacceptable cause. The idea of a *multiverse* has not been supported by experimental data, although in contrast to the first hypothesis, this one may possibly be demonstrable on a mathematical level. The principal philosophical criticism of this second hypothesis is that it does not respect the logical principle known as Occam's razor, according to which we may not postulate useless entities and complicated hypotheses must be avoided when unsupported by experience. Among explanations not based on verifiable and empirical data, logic imposes on us to select the simplest explanation. Another serious weakness of the idea of the *multiverse* derives from observational data that suggests our Universe is open, expanding, and in continuous evolution, which seriously contrasts with the idea of a self-enclosed cycle within a series.

Lastly, the third possibility postulates that behind the *fine-tuning* of the Universe there must be a project. This idea can be formulated based on the weak formulation of the anthropic principle, and does not necessarily imply either a theist valence or one of purpose in the sense of the strong formulation (see above). It certainly does, however, incline toward positing the existence of an intelligent mind, which some identify with a cosmic mind or an immanent intelligence, with which human beings may establish a *colloquy* only through mathematics, the sole means of contact between ourselves and it.

This hypothesis, which clearly represents an openness toward the concept of Logos, has met the consensus of scientists in various fields, some of whom are religious and some who are not.[152] Like the other two hypotheses, the last is merely a philosophical conjecture, unsupported by scientific or experimental proofs, and so cannot be tendentiously passed off as scientific knowledge. The most interesting aspect of the idea of a purposeful project inherent in existence is that it evokes a non-deterministic intentionality, a dynamic in which diverse agents involved in the project have a true, effectual freedom of action and choice.

Personally, I prefer the third hypothesis to the other two. Presupposing a purpose in existence seems to justify the rationality of the real, finding a meaning in it, but without establishing modes and times for the achievement of a goal. It leaves space for freedom and creativity but events, pathways, and results remain indeterminate. Among the supporters of this strong formulation stand theologians, philosophers, and scientists such as physicist Paul Davies, who began as a skeptic but now embraces the idea that an intelligent mind may have originated and now governs the Universe. Without such an origin, he asks, how can we explain the way nature has laws that lead from gases without characteristics to life, including consciousness and intelligence?[153] Another such scientist is Freeman Dyson, an eminent quantum physicist and mathematician, who explains,

From the existence of these physical and astronomical coincidences I come to the conclusion that the Universe is an extraordinarily hospitable location as a possible habitat for living creatures. And since I am a scientist accustomed to the modes of thought and language of the Twentieth century rather than the Eighteenth, I do not claim that the architecture of the Universe demonstrates the existence of God. I claim only that the architecture of the Universe is coherent with the hypothesis that the mind has an essential role in its functioning.[154]

The idea of an intentional project as the fount of existence entails to a greater degree the idea of a purpose and meaning than it does a Creator (although obviously a Creator cannot be excluded). Anthony Flew, another philosopher known for his radical shift from militant atheism to deism during the final period of his life, considers the anthropic principle "when properly formulated, the most popular and intuitively plausible argument in favor of the existence of God."[155] From his point of view, the correct formulation is the one proposed by Aristotle: God is a transcendent rational mind, the first cause of all reality. For my part, I can only say that the thought of an intelligent mind seems not far from Pareyson's idea of an originary liberty as an expression of a will that willed itself into existence.

Interpreting intelligent life

> In this inexhaustible and really quite unlikely Universe, humankind is not content simply to reproduce itself and die like other living beings. Humans do many other things—but above and before all else, they think. What is thinking? It is having an idea of oneself and the world around us. Who creates such an idea? As far as we know, the answer is that in the immensity of the Universe, only one individual, minute to the point of non-existence creates such an idea: me, that is, we. There is a greater distance between the Universe and the person thinking it than there is between a grain of sand and the ocean. But the grain of sand, less than nothing, is capable of the unheard of miracle of thinking itself and thinking of everything.[156]

What are we made of? We share approximately 40 percent of our DNA with the banana, too little to be equal to a banana. But we have in common 98 percent of our DNA with the African anthropomorphs. What makes us different from them? We know ourselves to be made of the same chemical elements that constitute everything; scientists are agreed on this fact. But there is something else in us. No one agrees about what this might be and where it comes from. Opinions differ diametrically and often stand in direct opposition.

Once upon a time it was certain and was considered absolutely evident that the human being consisted of a material, mortal body and an immaterial, immortal soul. Few people speak explicitly about the soul today, preferring to say that within us there is a spiritual *aspect* conducive to consciousness and awareness, that is, to the realm of the *mental*, of the brain and neuronal activity. Philosopher Richard Swinebourne is among the few who are unafraid to use the word soul, claiming that it coincides with consciousness. He specifies,

> Consciousness. . . cannot be the property of a simple body, of a material object. It must be the property of something different, connected to the body; and to that something else I will give the traditional name of soul.[157]

Naturally, since Swinbourne is expressing an opinion rather than making a scientific observation, his claim is subject to doubt, but neuroscientists distinguish clearly the brain and its neurons from consciousness. Consciousness is not, in fact, reducible to the stimuli that the brain sends, and should be understood rather as a "cognitive interpretation" of those neural stimuli.[158]

No one has yet been able to obtain a deep understanding of consciousness. Although differing quite a bit in details, opinion is substantially divided between those who think that consciousness (and mankind's spiritual inclination, of which consciousness could be a manifestation) is simply a product of the evolution of matter and the influence of culture, and those who, on the other hand, believe that consciousness belongs to a reality of a different order. This different order is the realm of the spirit, however much it may indeed be connected with matter and culture. For those of the first viewpoint, everything is matter, and all things derive from matter. For the others, something else, something that has an immaterial nature, exists alongside matter.

At this point the discourse becomes delicate, and before continuing we should recall that we find ourselves in the realm of philosophical speculation, open to doubt, in which only the internal logic of reasoning and a sensible overall design can incline listeners to prefer one position over another.

For centuries no one doubted the dualist nature of reality: it was considered obvious that spirit and matter were different substances, with the first animating the second. [159]

Everyone reputed that an individual's personal experience itself naturally led to that conclusion.

Like a malicious genie, science has demonstrated, however, that the separation between the material and the immaterial is much more complex than it may intuitively seem. The traditional terminology adopted to debate the question has become obsolete. In the current moment, the prevailing tendency seems to be that reality is essentially material, and intelligent biological life is inscribed in matter like an inborn potentiality.[160]

Biochemist Christian de Duve expresses this idea when he affirms that primordial matter is intrinsically endowed with *vital force*. In this sense, life would be seen as a property of matter.[161] But just when everyone seemed settled on this position and the idea of spirit—as a reality independent of matter, whatever that might mean—had been nearly abandoned, quantum physics came along to reshuffle the cards once again, with its discovery of the fundamental (although certainly mysterious) role of an entity as undeniably immaterial as information.

The first to suggest that the notion of information could be the best, most effective way to comprehend the world was physicist John Wheeler, a pupil of Niels Bohr and friend of Albert Einstein. He was convinced that if you look at reality in its true essence, it is nothing but a network of information in which every element is connected to all the others, to the point that it is possible to say quite literally that the Universe is *relation*. Wheeler expressed his idea with a formula that became quite famous in the world of science: *it from bit*: reality from information.

Genetics too seems to offer significant support to Wheeler's intuition, since DNA and RNA, the molecular structures of the cells of living organisms, are in the final analysis extraordinary systems for the transmission of information. It remains true, in any case, that the information must be transmitted by supporting structures (which merely seem to be almost immaterial), and that we still have no idea about the original source of information itself. This renders the whole question still more intriguing.

Making a sharp separation between the physical and the mental leads ultimately to a conviction that everything is material.[162] However, this leaves unexplained all those aspects of our experience that do not fit perfectly into one or the other category. In particular, an area that remains to be clarified is the passage from the electrochemical impulses in the brain to our sensations and feelings.[163]

Swinbourne's choice of introducing into discourse a semantics traditionally connected to the concept of the spirit—whose immaterial substance would be the mental life that includes and crosses boundaries of the physical and the cultural—allows us a new, speculative comprehension of elements as diverse as feeling, experience, thought, and purpose, which although linked to the brain still stand apart from it, in a condition which has still not found a satisfactory explanation:

> My spirit is the essential part of me. . . the essential part of the human person. . . You have left something extremely important out of the history of the world if you only tell the story of which physical events were produced because of other physical events.[164]

Effects on freedom

Disciplines such as astrophysics and biology have a natural inclination to think in terms of totalities—the Universe, life—and to formulate different "cosmo-visions". Well before these fields of research took form, however, human beings conceived and imagined many different versions of the origin and development of the world and life. In the next chapter we will dwell especially on how these questions are represented in the Bible, which has provided modes and tools that have deeply influenced thinking in the western world.

Before moving on, however, we should take a moment to consider how different interpretations of the origin of the world have affected the role and destiny of the concept of freedom. Diverse conceptions of mankind have been elaborated according to whether reality is held to be composed solely of matter or whether there also exists a transcendent spiritual or mental nature (whatever that might mean) which encompasses all reality. Limiting ourselves to pointing out only a few essential points, we may say that the kernel of our discourse is a strong hypothesis concerning the role of liberty in the dual dimensions of being (that is, metaphysics and interpretation) and becoming (in the evolution of history). Readers can refer to the bibliography for more thorough treatments of these themes, but they should be forewarned that they stand at the beginning of a path of study whose end I frankly admit I cannot see.

As we've said, diverse opinions on the origin of the world, with the world intended as *everything that exists*, can be roughly organized into three distinct categories: that it originated by *chance*, by *necessity*, or due to the *will* of an intelligent mind. We shall briefly examine the basic consequences that can be drawn from each of the three hypotheses.

There is little doubt that attributing the origin of existence to chance provides an unsatisfactory answer, because it tends to avoid rather than resolve the problem. Resorting to chance as an explanation fails to bring clarity to the origin of the Universe and does not even explain biological evolution, in which we see in action elements identifiable both as forms of freedom—such as choice and the unexpected—and natural law. But the principal reason why the hypothesis of randomness is unconvincing is that, if it were truly the controlling principle, then reality would be entirely incomprehensible, unpredictable, and ungovernable. Instead, we recognize the existence of laws that guarantee the regularity and measurability of phenomena which allow for most of our technological, biological, and scientific knowledge. If everything occurred by pure chance, we could never understand how anything works, and the world—granted that it could even exist in such conditions—would be absolute chaos. It is interesting to note that the most ancient myths of all humankind narrate the defeat of chaos by the gods, who then give order to the Universe precisely as a bulwark against the feared return of chaos. To say that the Universe arose by chance is frankly the same as saying that we don't know how it came about.

The second possibility is that there is a principle of necessity in the origin of the world, without which—given the physical and chemical premises of the Universe—it could not exist as it does. This solution, however, simply shifts the question backward to the problem of what determined the birth of this Universe and its laws. The Universe, in turn, must be the product of something preceding it and its laws. Some argue, in fact, that behind the laws that regulate the cosmos there must be some sort of super-law. From our viewpoint, this doesn't solve anything; it merely shifts the whole question of the unknown onto the hypothesized super-law.

In any case, even if we admit that the world is necessarily and inevitably what it is as a natural effect of the physics and chemistry of the Universe, its point of departure still remains a mystery. Above all, given the extremely precise calibration of all its parameters, we would have to consider the Universe's development as the outcome of a terribly rigid determinism. But if this were the case, even within the limits of our own Universe, the future would be entirely predictable, a situation contradicted by both experience and scientific evidence in both physics and biology, as we have previously discussed. Like the principle of chance, therefore, the principle of necessity also not only doesn't explain enough, but still more, leaves no space for freedom at any level, a restriction that renders it philosophically weak. It's quite clear that if every event and phenomenon took place within a rigid deterministic framework, we would be forced to conclude that freedom, and all that the concept implicates for human beings, is nothing but a misleading, subjective illusion.

I don't believe that, nor is there any cogent basis for this interpretation. On the contrary, it seems to me that the real functioning of the world, which we have somewhat superficially reconstructed in the preceding pages, inclines us to recognize liberty as one of the factors in the development of the Universe and of life, whose story is the result of an interaction among natural laws, random events, adaptation, and choices which may have been good or bad. Although necessary *natural causes* do exist, the relation among all the dynamics of reality remains unpredictable. It would have been impossible for all the dynamics in play to have resulted in an outcome that was inevitable and predictable from the very beginning.

We are left with the third hypothesis, which imagines an intelligent mind or intentionality as the course of all reality. Like the two preceding hypotheses, this is one that cannot be demonstrated, nor does it claim to be demonstrable, but it is reasonable, elegant, and has explanatory value. And it is clearly the most compatible of the three with Pareyson's vision of will as the absolute first and primeval freedom, which must have permeated all reality in various ways and measures, leaving its traces everywhere. To aid us in grasping this idea we might consider the analogy with gravity, which Einstein imagines not as a force that acts *within* space, but as something that *coincides* with space itself.[165] We might think similarly about freedom: it does not simply act on reality, but rather is an essential part of it. It belongs to the structure of reality, constituting its weft, as gravity does for space. To eliminate freedom would dissolve reality; there could be no reality without it, because freedom is the fundamental law of its realization. As Pareyson says, being and freedom coincide.

Another important advantage of the hypothesis of an intentional mind is the fact that it does not deny *a priori* any of the elements we have witnessed in operation in the evolution of the Universe and life—chance, necessity, freedom, contingency— which continually intersect and influence one another in the construction of reality. The world, in this hypothesis, is comprehensible because its physical structure is determined by the necessary laws of nature. It is not, however, predictable, because there is never only one possible reaction to any situation, because every moment is an interweaving of random chance, circumstances, and the freedom of the agents involved. An originary mind/will would make sense of the rationality that makes the world comprehensible and the freedom that renders it unpredictable. The Jesuit astronomer Father George Coyne, longtime director of the Specola Vaticana (1978-2006), a strong opponent of the concept of *intelligent design* because it "diminishes God, degrading him to the status of engineer", sees the matter this way:

> God hoped that we would one day come into existence. He may have prayed that we become a living reality. But he could not have rendered this outcome inevitable, because he created a Universe which did not determine us solely through the process of necessity. . . In his infinite freedom, God continually creates a world that reflects this freedom at every level of the evolutionary process through ever greater complexity.[166]

The *cosmo-visions*, as we have said, respond to the desire to reflect on the origin and becoming of the world in search of a functional explanation of reality and its dynamics, in order to imagine whether and what meaning it might have. Our experience, supported by evidence, tells us that there is a direction in evolution moving from one stage to another: from the small, simple cell to a larger, more complex one, from the monocellular organism to a multicellular one, from a basic consciousness to ever higher, more complex levels of knowledge and self-awareness, and so on.

Becoming and transformation have to do with time, the only dimension of space that cannot be traversed in two directions; it goes only one way.[167] The line of time proceeds only forward, because once something happens, it cannot turn back; *it cannot not have happened*, and its effects cannot be cancelled out. We know this from experience and, for the moment at least, time travel is something we find only in the movies. No one has ever gone into the past or future to modify them, and scientists are generally in agreement that it will never be possible to do so. For us, time flows, and everything flows with it; but towards what? And most of all, why? Is it directed toward some end, some goal? And who are we in all this? Are we merely the most advanced product of evolution, at least for now?

In recent times, after the arrogant triumphalism of the preceding centuries, we have progressively re-oriented our image of ourselves, and now think of ourselves not just as animals like the others (which we are) but as the worst of animals. The ferocity and invasiveness of human beings has relegated their intelligence and uniqueness to the background. Our species has a curious tendency to be *extremist* and vacillating. We are still animals like many others, but we also have characteristics and capacities that are unique, and this *superiority* grants us not rights over other species, but duties and an immense responsibility. Is this a simplistic way to see things? Perhaps.

The question becomes particularly urgent when thinking about the meaning of human life, different from all other species, about which we speculate because we are aware of ourselves and our individual destiny, which that death awaits us. Not only do we die like all living things, but we know we do for our entire lives. This renders life extremely precious in our eyes, but also makes it seem somehow senseless. All life is learning, they say: but what's the point, if we are destined for death no matter what, and everything we have learned with all our intelligence and experience will die with us?

We attempt to relieve this existential grief by finding meaning in our lives, in our learning and suffering, in our struggle with the world and ourselves to become better people. Psychology has made it quite clear that what gives us the greatest anguish is not so much the experiences we have, but the impossibility of finding meaning in them. Finding a meaning in life is of fundamental importance for we human beings. It is this desire, so strong as to seem a need, that makes us different from other living things, and it seems to have something to do with consciousness. We have already said that we still do not know what consciousness is. Some maintain that it and everything we perceive as spiritual, mental, and intellectual life, is a refined product of evolutionary and neurological processes; that is, of the chemistry of the brain.[168] Those who hold this position deduce that free will—the form of freedom peculiar to human beings—is nothing but the way in which we perceive and translate chemical mechanisms. Others consider consciousness a still unsolved mystery "*of* matter. The richness and mystery of existence are hidden in the freedom *of* matter, not in the freedom *from* matter. . ."[169] Consciousness would thus be potentiality intrinsic in matter, which has required everything that has happened and all the time it took to develop itself. Perhaps we are the consciousness of a Universe that obeys the same dynamics everywhere, the same laws, and has perhaps the same objectives. Perhaps thanks to us the Universe is aware of itself, so we can feel reassured, and not think of ourselves as shipwreck survivors or curious aliens, because, "every time we feel provoked to lift our gaze toward the firmament and meditate on the majestic beauty of the Universe, we are in reality nothing but the Universe meditating on itself."[170]

It could be that the purpose of the Universe and of all evolution has been to develop intelligent and conscious life. Such is the opinion of theologian Vito Mancuso, according to whom the Universe is directed not so much specifically toward the human being, but toward the intelligent being:

> There is a goal in evolution and this is the *sapiens-sapientia*. Not *homo* . . . but *sapiens*. *Homo* is the contingent supporting structure that evolution has been able to produce through a history worked up out of logos and chaos; *sapiens-sapientia* is the goal, which remains far from having been reached by the current state of mankind, which is often hardly *sapiens* at all.[171]

Mancuso adds that rather than *Homo sapiens*, the result of evolution may have been *Saurus sapiens* (in English we might say "dino-sapiens"), and observes that evolution can be interpreted in three ways: as a process without any goal; as a process with both a pre-established goal and a fixed path (such is the view of fundamentalist creationists who, pretending to accept evolution, in fact deny it); or as a process with an aim but without a pre-established path to that goal. The last of these is the approach to evolution that Mancuso proposes calling *creation*.[172] This is the perspective from which Mancuso identifies *sapiens-sapientia* as the goal, while the path toward it is represented by the multiple factors we have discussed, such as natural law, contingency, and choice.

The mutation that governs evolution is not blind, because it is a "growing accumulation of complexity"[173] impelled toward "the growth of intelligence into knowledge, which is a particular form of intelligence, the highest: the goodness of intelligence."[174] A fully aware, just, and good mind could be the goal of evolution, the direction in which it moves. We could say that the objective of evolution, seen as creation, is the spirit, understood as a freedom that freely chooses the good.[175]

Again we encounter the dualism of spirit and matter, quite difficult to escape from.[176] To resolve this dilemma Mancuso introduces a nuance that may seem merely semantic but is in fact substantial: the very nature of reality, he claims, is not *dualistic* but *dual*, a fact that science itself compels us to recognize:

> Physics today leads us to see our Universe as dual, that the original being/energy is expressed in two structurally relational modes, such as energy-matter and energy-force. It follows that, against dualism, we must insist that there is a single, unique nature . . . and that this unique nature subsists from its origin in two distinct modes, the evolution of which leads us reasonably to speak of matter and spirit, body and soul, world and God.[177]

In Mancuso's vision (which recalls that of Pareyson in diverse aspects and emphases) the ultimate goal of evolution/creation is freedom, which he understands in its definitive expression as love. Personally, on this point I feel closer to Pareyson, who sees in freedom the cause, rather than the goal, of existence. Love could be the primary impulse that motivated liberty, and the goal—possible, hoped for, but uncertain—toward which all existence yearns, the highest evolutionary stage.

To conclude this chapter on problems in the interpretation of reality, and in particular on the conceptual implications of our initial hypothesis, I would argue that the idea of an intelligent mind at the origin of all existence is coherent and compatible with the hypothesis that freedom is an energy that manifests as a power, from whose activity matter and spirit evolve in all their forms. Just as scientists think that the originating forces from which all reality arose—gravity, electromagnetism, strong and weak interaction—derived from a single force, we can imagine something similar with regard to freedom. All the existent forms of freedom, including human freedom, derive from an absolute *primeval freedom*, such that human freedom remains indissolubly linked to that primeval manifestation.

Like Hans Jonas who we have already cited, many scholars have called this original power *divine liberty*, and they give the being/force/will from which all things flow the traditional name of God. Within this dynamic, humankind cannot be reduced to its biological dimension because we recognize in ourselves a *surplus* whose nature we can describe in many ways.[178] The result is creativity, or co-creativity, which positions human beings in a real, although not unlimited, state of freedom.[179]

Appendix to Chapter Five

A Universe for life?

Weak anthropic principle or prebiotic conditions.

What relation can we hypothesize between the Universe and biological life? Is our Universe favorable to life or is it made for life? Apparently fatuous at first glance, the question is in fact subtle and intriguing. Tanzella-Nitti puts it into focus very neatly: "In the first place, the evolution of the Universe manifests itself with a strong character of unity. The four laws of fundamental interaction and their a-dimensional constants determine the physics of the Universe and how it will evolve much more than the single events that will accompany its development in time. The Universe is certainly not a deterministic machine, as maintained by mechanicism in the 18th and 19th centuries, as we know from today's physics, which has amply informed us of the mathematical unpredictability of a good part of its phenomena . . . At the same time, however, neither does the Universe present itself as a jumble of disconnected parts devoid of unifying rationality, remnants of reality whose capacity for emergence and autopoesis is entrusted purely to the accidental interactions that mark out its history. Scientific data at the base of the "biotic conditions" (as derived from the weak anthropic principle) show, on the contrary, that the essential characteristics of the physics of the Universe are conceptually determined, and that the creativity that accompanies the morphological complexification, although open and mathematically unpredictable, is implicitly conditioned by founding properties that are never contradicted. The origin of this creativity is to be found temporally in the primitive phenomenology involved in the formation of space-time, of the field of radiation, and lastly of matter, in both its hadron and lepton components. In the second place, it is clear that biology and human life depend greatly on the entire history of the Universe (here we use the term history in an imprecise, analogical sense). There was nothing superfluous in this history. The long epochs that separate us from the Big Bang, without which the stars would not have been able to synthesize and then transmit into space the chemical overflow necessary to form organic molecules, were needed so that we could be "here" and "now". As a consequence, even the dimensions of the Universe and the unbounded quantity of matter it contains seem to some degree indispensable for the presence of life, even if this life exists only on planet Earth. The radius of the Universe is in fact proportional to the time of expansion, and all the matter it contains (in theory, it could have contained still more, since the majority of it transformed into radiation in the earliest phases of the cosmos) depends on delicate balances among nature's constants. There does not seem to be anything superfluous in the cosmos; everything that exists appears to be strictly necessary to host life. Thirdly, the (necessary but not sufficient) conditions that render life possible appear as "originary conditions". The influence that a certain number of more or less random events may have had in the formation, for example, of our terrestrial habitat, was basically inferior, as concerns the development of life, to the factors contained in the initial conditions of the Big Bang by the "fixed values" of nature's constants and other fundamental physical constants. What we intend to stress here . . . [is] . . . the scientific datum of the original, non-evolutionary character of those values . . . Compared with biological evolution, the "biotic conditions" suggest that the paradigm of natural selection and the capacity to adapt to the environment cannot be the only governing rule in operation throughout the long chain of circumstances that led to the appearance and development of life. This is fundamentally in agreement with the tenets of contemporary biology, which by now is accustomed to flanking the Darwinian paradigm with other developmental and evolutionary factors." (Cfr. Tanzella-Nitti, *Dizionario*, cit.)

Religious implications of the anthropic principle.
     The strong anthropic principle has also led to a religious version of determinism in the U.S. that has sparked a movement known as Creationism. Creationism rejects evolution, preferring a literal reading of the Scriptures. In a more moderate form called "Intelligent Design", evolution is considered to be an instrument invented and directed by God in a project whose culmination is humankind. This can be considered an opinion, but the problem arises when—as religious movements have done in the U.S.—it is championed as a scientific theory that should be taught "as a subject matter in public schools in place of the theory of evolution, without anyone protesting against the violation of the American Constitution, which prohibits religious teachings in public institutions" (Francisco J. Ayala, *Il dono di Darwin*, 193). Telmo Pievani observes, "Believing that a god used the laws of nature and the mechanisms of evolution

to carry out his will—as does the director of the Human Genome Research Institute, Francis Collins—may seem rather implausible to others, but it is innocuous to evolutionary reasoning and cannot be refuted by scientific data. It is a philosophy of "Newtonian" compromise that Darwin himself touched on repeatedly. In any case, it is a doctrine totally distinct from Intelligent Design, which would like to be recognized as fully scientific and replace evolutionary explanations." He concludes quite rightly that, "Intelligent Design is first of all a debasement of religious feeling through forced rationalization, a maladroit and failed attempt to translate faith into a conceptual network or even a scientific theory, distorting and violating the nature of faith. It is the child of a fearful religiosity, more aggressive in reaction to growing distress, which seeks pseudo-scientific justification for a dogma of faith. . . (Telmo Pievani, *Creazione senza Dio*, 97, 129) Ayala also totally rejects any scientific validity to Intelligent Design, noting that the very "imperfection of the structures reveals the existence of evolution and disproves the claims of so-called Intelligent Design." He adds, "I maintain that 1) Intelligent Design is implausible from a scientific viewpoint; 2) without value for a religious viewpoint, because it attributes unacceptable characteristics to the Creator." (Francisco Ayala, *Il dono di Darwin alla scienza*, cit., 134, 191) A fitting specification in this discussion comes from Tanzella-Nitti, who observes, "The idea of being able to recognize the presence of an intelligent design in nature as proof of the existence of a Creator has accompanied a good part of human thought . . . The anthropic principle, or the 'biotic conditions' associated with it bring to light only the coherence, coordination, and inter-relations present in the structure and evolution of the cosmos. These cannot be employed directly and without further reflection as a demonstration of an intelligent design, nor can they demonstrate the existence of a necessary and absolute teleology toward the appearance of life and mankind." (Tanzella-Nitti, *Il principio antropico e le sue implicazioni telogiche*, cit.)

Monism or dualism?

Philosophers and scientists have asked themselves since ancient times what quantities and types of substances the world is made of. Is it composed of only one substance or many? These are the alternatives of monism and dualism. Monism can be materialistic when it attributes all things, including spiritual expressions, to physical matter, while it can be spiritualistic or pan-psychic when it views every aspect of nature, including material objects, as the manifestation of a soul or a mind intrinsic to matter. Obviously we are in the field of speculation and interpretation, such that no position can be unquestionable. Francisco Ayala specifies, "Science is methodologically materialistic, or rather methodologically naturalistic. I prefer this second adjective because the term 'materialism' often indicates a metaphysical conception of the world, a philosophy according to which nothing exists but the material world, nothing but what our senses perceive. . . science does not necessarily imply metaphysical materialism. Scientists who claim that science excludes the validity of any knowledge beyond science commit a 'category error'; they confuse scientific method and authority with the metaphysical implications of science. Methodological naturalism affirms that scientific knowledge has precise confines, and not that everything it says in every field is valid." (F. Ayala, *Il dono di Darwin*, 245) John Searle considers it an error to utterly separate the physical from the mental, explaining his view in these terms: "The traditional conception that reality is physical is erroneous in at least three points:" 1) the terminology is not exact, in that there are aspects that do not fit precisely in the distinction between physical and mental; 2) contemporary science has rendered obsolete or very difficult the distinction between physical and mental. Think for example of the electron, which is a point of mass-energy; 3) lastly, "it is profoundly wrong to suppose that a central task of ontology is to ask ourselves what types of things exist in the world, rather than asking ourselves what must take place in the world for our empirical claims to be true." He concludes that given "the incoherence of dualism, it is clear that monism and materialism are equally in error. While dualists, asking what types of objects and properties exist in the world, have identified two, the monists have identified one only: they have both fallen into the same error, which consists precisely in having attempted such a qualification. . . I maintain that materialism—which begins with the acceptance of the Cartesian categories—should be seen above all as a particular form of dualism. If a coherent dualist takes those categories seriously—the mental and the physical, the mind and the body—he or she will end up embracing materialism, which is in a certain sense the finest flower of dualism. . ." (cfr. John R. Searle, *La riscoperta della mente*, esp. 41-42)

6. *Freedom in the Bible*

Why talk about the Bible?

The hypothesis that freedom belongs so structurally to the texture of being that without it the cloth of which the world is made would vanish, and nothing of what exists could be, has led us to seek traces and dynamics of freedom both in physical and biological matter. We have then considered how conceiving of freedom as a true element of reality or, on the contrary, as an illusion of the human mind, can radically impact our conception of the world and life.

We will now dwell in particular on one of the interpretations of the world, that of the Bible. To begin with I will adopt and share with readers the exhortation of Bible scholar Carmine de Sante, who, stressing the urgency to return to an interrogation of what religion is and, particularly in the west, what is Biblical religion, invites us to do it with a free spirit, without prejudices either for or against.[180] Since the conception of God always reflects a correlative conception of humankind and the world, when speaking in the Bible of God, we also speak of mankind, its experiences, and its thought.[181] Given this fact, the objective of the reading we offer here is to understand whether the idea of freedom emerges at the roots of the culture we belong to, and what that idea is.

Considering the Bible in terms of freedom outside a strictly religious discourse, therefore, should not arouse perplexity. Opposing God to freedom, and even more, religion to freedom belongs to a contemporary patrimony of commonplaces. It is a misleading direction, but one whose motivation is not hard to understand.[182] But the close connection between the Bible and freedom has been stated incisively by Abraham Joshua Heschel, one of the most important Jewish philosophers of the Twentieth century, who said, "The most magnificent idea that Judaism dares to formulate is that the cause of every being is freedom, not necessity."[183]

Anyone searching in the Bible for a discussion of freedom will not find it, and yet freedom is the Bible's essential element, the kernel of the story not only upon which Israel has constructed its national identity; it is the foundation of monotheistic faith, still shared today by a considerable percentage of humanity. The fact that those same faiths born from a Biblical root, today as in the past, sometimes repudiate and fail to recognize freedom among their vital values, even fighting against it, does not mean that freedom is not part of what they are. Rather, it is a consequence of the inadequacy of human beings and that subtle, devastating form of fear born of ignorance, which we seem to be incapable of freeing ourselves from.

The idea of freedom, like many other ideas that have become a common patrimony of modern culture and thought—like fraternity, equality, justice—emerged in a religious context. For most of history, religion has permeated every aspect of life. The beginning of our conceptual world took shape in that distant setting, and has come down to us through the mediation of Christianity and its hybridization with Greek philosophy. Even scientific culture, which we often believe to be antithetical to a biblical conception of the world, is deeply indebted to it, as Albert Einstein wrote in 1948:

> Although it's true that scientific results are completely independent of moral or religious considerations, the individuals who have most contributed to making great discoveries for science had a full, purely religious conviction that in our Universe there was a rationally analyzable perfection. If this conviction had not been impassioned, if those who sought to know had not been inspired by the *amor Dei intellectualis* of Spinoza, it is unlikely they would have been able to dedicate themselves tirelessly to it, the only way of achieving great results.[184]

Biblical stories always have two protagonists: mankind (many men and women, and sometimes even animals and plants) and God, the name which, as Karl Jaspers says, has always meant "that which transcends the world and precedes it."[185] Or, in the words of philosopher Salvatore Natoli, "*that name* which humanity has given to the gap between the infinite and the limit in which it finds itself."[186]

Trascendence and *immanence*, *infinity* and *limit*, *mankind* and *God*: different ways of expressing a contact point, a border that joins and separates the known and unknown, a belonging differently to the same adventure, which Abraham Joshua Heschel expresses thus:

> Behind the mind and matter, behind order and relations, the freedom of God affirms itself. The inevitable is not eternal. Every constriction is the result of a choice. A portion of this exemption from necessity hides in the folds of the human spirit.[187]

Because of this, divine liberty stands alongside human liberty in the Bible, such that it is impossible to understand one without the other (cfr. Jonas).

The interdependence between God and freedom appears obvious to some but incomprehensible, even contradictory, to others.[188] In response to their objections, it would be tempting to cite Luigi Pareyson's observation that *God is freedom*, but taken on its own this statement might lead one to think that *freedom is God*. This would be a grave mistake, however, because in this case the commutative property does not function: by changing the order of the factors, the result changes, and what's more, it is wrong.

Returning to Pareyson's idea as explained in Chapter One, we see that at the origin of everything there was an act of absolute freedom, a choice in favor of existence made by a transcendent will that was not merely human, but somehow encompassed all reality. The will presupposes a *persona*, not necessarily a human being, but clearly something not inferior to a human being.[189] Diverse scientists imagine this entity as an intelligence or a mathematical mind which in some still unknown way,originates and orders matter and energy. Other scientists and philosophers attribute to this will an ulterior attribute which they characterize as "the reality of sense beyond information and meaning."[190] In this case we can also call this *God*, as suggested—as we have seen—by Jaspers and Natoli.

When we identify this noun—as a generic term rather than a proper noun—as possessing a will as real as our own—free, creative, and equipped with sensibility—the noun *God* implicates that the gap between ourselves and the infinite is not only a natural question, such as the difference separating inert matter from biological matter, but refers to the existence of an *Other* that transcends the world while interacting with it. This is the biblical sense of the word *God*.[191]

From this perspective, it seems to me that God and freedom are conceptually inseparable.

In fact, conceiving of a divine reality whose nature does not include freedom, with freedom permeating the dynamic of the phenomenology of world, would impede us from imagining God as a possible reality, relegating that conception instead to something like a dream or a desire. By definition, a God without freedom could not be God, because it would be subject to something else, and thus not free.

In the same way, a free God who is the source of a reality that negates freedom to creation would be *unthinkable*, because if freedom belonged to God's nature, that same freedom would in some way spill over to a degree into the reality emanating from God. Otherwise reality could not be considered an emanation of God; without this, there would be no God.

If, finally, we wished to save the concept of God but deny the existence of freedom, we would be compelled to think of God as a malignant form of transcendence, source of every aspect of evil, which would stamp the world with its own malignancy. The good would be non-existent or impossible. This dark vision is negated by the clear evidence of beauty and goodness in the world and in human nature.

On the other hand, conceiving of liberty while simultaneously rejecting any evocation of a transcendent reality would lead ultimately to attributing divine status to freedom itself. Freedom would become a sort of impersonal idol reigning over all, a blender capable of mincing reality into an indistinguishable chaos. This idea contradicts the astonishing order of nature, which—although always at risk of collapsing into chaos, as shown by the precarious stability of the Higgs boson—seems to conduct an immense, harmonious dance in which every single entity, from the infinitely small to the infinitely large, moves in a mutating, precarious, but perfect equilibrium.

From all that has been said here, I find it reasonable, interesting, and even necessary to seek evidence of freedom in the biblical conception of the world.

What is the Bible?

Although it speaks of God, the Bible is not a book of theology, because it doesn't reason about God; rather, it tells of his actions and his relations with the world.

Still less is it a book about science, so there's no sense in seeking *scientific* truths in it, nor in expecting it to answer questions of a scientific type. Different from what happens in Greek culture, the biblical man shows no scientific curiosity toward the natural world. In biblical Hebrew there is no term to correspond to the Greek word *fusis* (nature). The world is observed and interpreted in terms of the knowledge of its era and Semitic sensibility, with nature understood as *creation*.

Through myths, history, and the beliefs of Israel, the complex and heterogeneous text of the Bible delineates a specific vision of the world and a precise idea of the nature of humanity and its condition. Israel does not *think* God, it has no *idea* of God; rather, Israel *has encountered* God, and in its sacred text it tells the story and hands down the memory of its experience with the divine.

From the conviction of the encounter with God comes the certainty that he is present—that he wants to be present—in human history; otherwise Israel would never have been able to meet him. And having encountered (or intuited) God, nothing could be more important than understanding what God is like. Understanding God through his actions and words (note that the same word is used in biblical Hebrew to indicate actions and words, meaning that the divine word always effectually impacts reality) is the most important task of any Israelite and the people of Israel. Due to this fact, hermeneutics has become the Judaic science *per excellence*, extraordinarily fruitful over the centuries for the religious and philosophical thought of the Mediterranean world.

Beyond being always efficacious, the divine world is superabundant with meaning, such that its interpretation is inexhaustible. The wisdom books express this with the formula *One thing God has spoken; two things have I heard.*[192] The same idea is expressed with a beautiful image passed down by the sages who describe the Bible as *written with black fire and white fire*: fire, because the word/action of God illuminates, scorches, burns and devours. Black fire is the color of the ink that writes the letters; white fire is the space between the letters, which is not merely blank, but is the margin left open to the interpretive labor of mankind, an integral part of divine revelation. Thus the Bible is the *word of God in the stories of mankind.*[193]

In the cultural universe of the Bible, humans do not perceive themselves as creatures crushed by subservience to God, but as interlocutors and collaborators with God. Divine revelation can arrive only as mediated through human narration, and is thus inevitably conditioned by the historical and cultural situation of the *narrators.* As long as there are intelligences capable of reading and interpreting it, the Bible will remain inexhaustible and always immediately relevant, unless the interest it demands drops away and it becomes, as Abraham Joshua Heschel feared, "a sublime answer, but we no longer know the question."[194]

The book of books. Brief notes on the text of the Bible

In biblical Hebrew, the concept of the superlative is expressed using a singular noun followed by the same noun in the plural, for example *Song of*

Songs, the title of a poetic wisdom book, means *the most beautiful song*, the most sublime, the absolute best; the *heaven of heavens*, the highest of all the heavens; the *Holy of Holies* is he who is the holiest of all, God himself. The Bible is called the *book of books* to say that it is the greatest, the most important of all, the book *per excellence*; in fact it is often referred to simply as *the Book*. At the origin of this denomination there is, however, also the fact that the Bible is a collection of many books in diverse genres: myths, historical chronicles, poetic texts, prophetic writings, theological treatises, letters, reports, legends, proverbs, mystical visions. Each genre has its own style, written by different, mostly unknown authors, in different languages: Hebrew, Aramaic, Greek. The individual texts were edited over the course of approximately a millennium, from the 8th century BCE to the 3rd century CE, based on much more ancient oral traditions coming from the 12th-11th centuries BCE. Each of these bears "the trace of a past earlier than any memory or history."[195] The fact that different, sometimes partially contradictory versions of the same episode are sometimes narrated seems to confirm the theory that the text originated from multiple sources long passed down orally, and only later collected into a unified account.[196]

The Bible is the sacred text of the Jewish and Christian religions and the text of both versions are identical. Any differences concern the prominence granted to the diverse components. The Jewish Bible consists of 46 books, while the Christian version consists of 73 because, in addition to the texts of the Judaic tradition that precede the story of Jesus which constitute the *Tanakh* or Old Testament, the Christian Bible also has a second part, the New Testament, which includes the four *Gospels*, the *Acts of the Apostles*, various *Letters*, and *Revelation* or the *Apocalypse* of John. These are the texts that recount the life and preaching of Jesus, the origin of the Christian churches, and the original foundations of Christian theology.[197]

The Jewish version of the Bible is called the *Tanakh*, an acrostic formed from the initial letters of the three parts it is composed of. The first and most sacred of all is the *Torah*, a word usually translated as *Law* but which more precisely evokes the concepts of *path* and *teaching*; another name for this is the *Pentateuch*.[198] The second part is called *Nevi'im*, which means *Prophets*, subdivided in turn into the *Former Prophets* and the *Latter Prophets*. The third section is called *Kethuvim*, or *Writings*.

In both the Jewish and the Christian versions, the books narrate events in chronological order, from the origins of the world until the exile into Babylon in the 6th century BCE for the *Tanakh-Pentateuch*, up to the end of Time (with the *Apocalypse*, or *Revelation*) in the Christian Bible. We know, however, that the composition of the *Tanak*, or *Old Testament*, was not chronological, in that the accounts of the most ancient events were not the first to be written down.[199]

In substance, four temporal phases are recognized in the composition of the Bible. The first is the era of the oral tradition, the true origin of the biblical tales; the second is the phase when the stories were transcribed; the third is when the various scrolls and papyri on which the accounts were written were unified into a single book; the final phase is when the definitive text was completed in the version we read today.

Because the accounts narrated are so distant in time, it is reasonable to doubt their reliability, except that we know the importance attributed to memorization in the era before the written word. Writing is a relatively recent invention, dating to only a few thousand years ago, meaning that a considerable part of history, the fundamental depository of knowledge and the guarantor of its passage from generation to generation, has been entrusted to memory.[200]

Once writing came into wide use, and especially after papyrus—far easier to manage than stone or wax tablets—became its primary medium, the sacred status accorded to collective memory shifted to the precise copying of texts. Important confirmation of this change came from the discovery of the Qumran scrolls, including several complete copies of books of the Bible (*Isaiah*, *Psalms*, *Habakkuk*) and numerous fragments of others dating to the 2nd century BCE. It thus became possible to read biblical transcriptions predating by a thousand years the versions heretofore available, which were from the 9th century CE. The Qumran *Isaiah* scroll and the 9th century edition were found to differ only by a letter here and there! The text had passed from generation to generation in virtually identical form for a thousand years. Why shouldn't we think that similarly precise transmission might not have been practiced during the preceding millennium?

Even if the editorial history of the books of the Bible has not been established in every particular, scholars agree that they are "the expression of an ancient civilization that, through a variegated inheritance, had a profound influence on western civilization."[201]

In sum, therefore, and in particular regarding the Pentateuch, it is held that its basis is an oral tradition dating to the 12th-11th century BCE. The cycles of stories that narrate the origins of the diverse tribal groups who would come to constitute *the children of Israel* were gathered and unified in a subsequent era (probably between the 8th and 6th centuries BCE) by mostly anonymous authors. The organization of all the materials into a single book must have taken place after the nation's return from its Babylonian Exile (in the 6th century) when, in order to reconstruct the identity of Israel and Judah, the community recuperated the ancient oral traditions to compose a coherent encompassing version of history and spiritual experience it embodied.

Moses and the exodus from Egypt

The Bible's quite particular conception of freedom is dyadic and dialogic; that is, always expressed as doubled between human freedom and divine freedom. This characteristic emerges prominently and with great richness of meaning in certain stories in the Pentateuch. The first of these recounts the words God directs to the Hebrews fleeing across the desert, when he proposes them an alliance based on their acceptance of the Decalogue. The second is the episode in which God speaks to Moses from the burning bush, revealing his Name. The third is the compelling invitation he makes to the patriarch Abraham to leave the land of his ancestors to go to a new land which the Lord will indicate to him. The fourth is the mythical account of creation and the brief sojourn of the first human couple in the Garden of Eden, which deals with the absolute freedom of God in its encounter with the equally absolute freedom of humankind. This final part of the discourse will lead us back around in a circle to the reflections by Pareyson that motivated this book.

Readers will have noted that the four episodes are listed in reverse chronological order; instead of following the order of the narration, we follow instead the order of composition. We shall take up first the most ancient of the written texts: the verses of the Decalogue are considered the most ancient nucleus of the Pentateuch, while the creation myth recounted in Genesis 1-3 is thought to be the most recent. This sequence will allow us to better follow the formation of the biblical physiognomy of freedom.

The Bible in its entirety, not merely the first five books, tells the story of a progressive liberation, of a gradually expanding awareness of the existence of freedom and the ineluctability of putting it to use or, in other words, the impossibility of avoiding it. Nevertheless, in the whole Pentateuch the word *freedom* or *liberty* appears only three times, and always in relation to the contrary condition of slavery. It's reasonable to imagine that the idea of freedom, historically speaking, may have come after the fearful experience of slavery, upon which the economic and social organization of the ancient world was based.[202]

Often completely impotent in the face of the forces of nature, the ancients saw the world as a place of incomprehensible mysteries, often terrifying or extremely dangerous. The most important thing, therefore, was safety, which only belonging to a group might provide.

The greatest of all fears was that primordial chaos might return to overcome a world that had established order only with the greatest effort. It is important to remember this, because this fear will play a role, as we shall see, in the conception of God found in Genesis. It is easy to imagine the fear of the return of chaos if we remember that we are speaking of the inhabitants of ancient Mesopotamia, the land between two rivers, and the recurrent flooding of the plain between the Tigris and Euphrates, especially in its southern estuary.

The ancients believed that only the gods could maintain order in the cosmos, and to gain their benevolence and preserve their wellbeing so they might defeat the power of chaos, people offered them food and honors.

For a long time the closest thing to freedom that humans could conceive was the idea of belonging to a strong social body and contributing one's labor to conserve the natural order of the world by serving one's god and king.

The first episode we will explore must have developed in a sociocultural context of this type: the flight of a large group of slaves, descendants of a Semitic clan of nomadic shepherds resident for several generations in Egypt. It has been observed that this may have been the first large-scale escape from slavery in history, and it marked (or was felt to be) a turning point, a change in mentality destined to profoundly affect the lives of its protagonists and their descendants.[203] In the memory of Israel, this was such an extraordinary event that only a divine intervention could have seen it through; how else to explain that a group of refugees including women, the aged, and children, without weapons and lost in the wilds, could overcome the power of Egypt? The epic, miraculous Exodus told in the Bible's second book became the divine saga of the birth of the nation of Israel. It is the story of a liberation.[204]

The events are well known. Joseph, eleventh of the patriarch Jacob's twelve sons, had become Vizier to the Pharoah in Egypt, thus gaining favor for the Jews who lived there. After Joseph's death, the Jews became what we'd call today an ethnic minority so numerous and influential that the Egyptians began to see them as a threat. Having never met Joseph, the new Pharoah did not honor the bonds of friendship and loyalty with his descendants and, fearful lest they ally with Egypt's enemies, he enslaved them. *Exodus* begins by describing the harsh oppression borne by the Jews, and then proceeds with God's summons to Moses to lead them out of Egypt, with the miraculous crossing of the Sea of Reeds (the actual translation of the Hebraic *Yam Suf*, usually identified as the *Red Sea*); the long wandering in the desert; the divine apparition near Mount Sinai (called, in other passages, Oreb); the giving of the *ten words* (the Decalogue); the covenant between God and all the peoples gathered at the foot of the mountain (Jewish and foreign refugees, men and women); and various laws and cultic norms that would hereafter regulate the life of Israel.

We encounter two particularly significant moments in this story: the first is the giving of the Decalogue; the second is the revelation of the Name of God. Once again, the narrative order would induce us to deal first with the matter of the Name, but following instead the order of composition, we will first discuss the Decalogue, which in fact contains the most ancient text in the entire Pentateuch: "*I am the Lord thy God, which have brought thee out of the land of Egypt, out of the house of bondage,*" followed by the Ten Commandments.[205]

Here for the first time we find the words of God addressed directly to the entire assembled populace: we can say that God presents himself to the people and the first thing he says of himself is that he *has freed* them. And since he wants these words to be repeated from father to son, since then and forever, this means that God wants to be forever remembered as the one who has liberated, as the liberator. Israel will build its spiritual and cultural identity on this memory of its origins. Its first, most ancient act of faith is to recall a liberation: *God has freed us from slavery.*

But why did God liberate them? This is an important question, because from the Jewish perspective the actions of God reveal God's nature. The story says that he freed the Jews because he saw their suffering (he is interested in the world) and he remembered (he is loyal) the pact sealed long ago with their fathers. Now he wants to renew the pact and wants the liberated Jews to serve him. What is the advantage in this for the Jews? Why flee from servitude (but also security) in Egypt to serve a God they had long since forgotten, who seemed to have neglected them for so long?[206]

Discovering the difference between serving God and serving Pharoah is the purpose of the long travail in the desert, during which the freed Jews must learn to *want* to be free. As philosopher Michael Walzer wrote, their long sojourn in the desert is not a period of wandering, but, "a march toward a goal, a moral progress, a transformation. . . The purpose is to teach the importance of the march and the discipline necessary for its success."[207] The difference between serving God and the Pharoah is in the alliance, which is "the political invention of the Book of Exodus . . . There is no precedent for pacts between God and entire people and treaties whose conditions are the very laws of morality."[208] The pact (*berith*) proposed is technically and formally the same as those stipulated between sovereigns of cities, on a level of parity, which does not mean that God and mankind are equal, "if equality is thoughtlessly taken to mean interchangeability, but on the level of dignity this pact places the two subjects on the same level. Creator and creature have equal dignity."[209]

What Israel does in this episode is a true revolution in the relationship between the human and the divine, and still another aspect of it is also completely new: its universality. Expressly by divine command, all the people are gathered at the foot of Sinai, the chiefs and the elderly, all the men and also all the women, the children and all the foreigners present in the fugitive camp. Everyone must listen and respond, because everyone must accept responsibility. In a totally tribal context, for the first time there is an intuition of the universal alliance between the divine and the human.

But freedom is difficult, as philosopher Emmanuel Levinas explains, because in order to be truly achieved in the world it must be desired and learned, and precisely because it is difficult the people must love it and be willing to pay a high price for it.[210] This difficulty is expressed in biblical language in the continuous lamentation of the refugees against Moses, whom they accuse of having liberated them only to leave them to die in the desert. In Egypt they may have been slaves, but at least they had meat and bread enough to fill their bellies.

The fact is that it's not enough to leave Egypt. The people must lift their gaze higher and cast it farther to see the *promised land*. They must desire much more than a full stomach to be free. The passage from the Pharoah's yoke to the bond of divine or moral law marks the birth of ethics, or rather the knowledge that only by subjecting themselves to the law does the exercise of liberty become concretely possible in a social grouping. But Israel goes beyond this, and through the story of the alliance with God and the events of the Exodus it delineates an entirely new ideal: the dream of becoming *a kingdom of priests and holy people*. To achieve this, "the only guarantee is rectitude."[211]

After having heard the Decalogue, the assembled host responds, "All that the Lord hath said we will do, and we will listen."[212] The phrasing sounds a bit strange, because we should listen before we act, but the order here is reversed: first we will do, then we will listen. Every detail has a purpose in the Bible, so this strange sequence must mean something. The most convincing interpretation is that inverting the two actions signifies that the Jews have been asked to do

something apparently incomprehensible, which they would be able to understand only in the act of doing of it. *Now* they do not know what freedom is,
nor what it entails, but by accepting the law they will come to understand as
events unfold. Through the Decalogue, therefore, Israel affirms freedom as an
ethical act, and for the first time discipline and justice are posited as corollaries
of freedom.

Among the ten commandments is the sanctification of the sabbath as a
day of total respite from all labor. This is a very important command which
implies a precise idea of the human condition. Repose, in fact, differentiates
the forced labor of the slave from that of the free individual. By affirming an
absolute right to repose the commandment proclaims the freedom of the human
being, whose labor resembles the free and creative activity of God, who labored
for six days but rested on the seventh.[213] The fact that the right to the repose of
the sabbath day is extended to all—slaves, animals, and even the land, which
must be left fallow every seven years—introduces and affirms freedom and the
dignity that accompanies it as an aspiration and right of every living thing.[214]

The Name of God

One of the most mysterious stories in the entire Old Testament is the one
that tells how God, speaking from a bush that burned without being consumed,
revealed himself to Moses, asking him to return to Egypt to liberate the Israel-
ites. Moses had fled from Egypt after having killed an Egyptian soldier to defend
a Jewish slave. Like almost all the major figures in the Bible, Moses at first gives
a poor impression of himself: he does not answer heroically, but responds to
God with reluctance, listing excuses and rationales to free himself from duty,
to the point that God loses his patience, at which Moses finally gives in.[215] He
asks the voice coming from the bush, however, in whose name he must say he
has been sent: "Behold, when I come unto the children of Israel and shall say to
them, The God of your fathers hath sent me unto you; and they shall say to me,
What is his name? what shall I say unto them?" (Exodus 3, 13).

What appears to be an obvious, simple question turns out to be much
more involved than it seems. In antiquity, in fact, a name was not considered
merely the most obvious way of identifying a person; it was believed to truly
contain the personality, destiny, and character of the person. This is why rites of
passage from childhood to adulthood in many archaic cultures include a change

of name, whether chosen by a shaman or by the person undergoing the passage. Asking God his name means being able to pray to him, to learn his will, and to interact with him; in this sense Moses's intention was to find out what kind of divinity God was and what kind of relationship he wished to establish with the people he was sending Moses to save.

In his wish to learn the divine name, however, Moses also had the less honest, more ambiguous aim of manipulating the divinity by using the power conferred by the magical use of the name itself. Such practices, common in antiquity, were based on the conviction that mankind could bend the gods to its will by invoking their name according to certain formulas. In a way, the person who knew the name of a god had that god in their hands (this was the basis of the power of the priestly caste). The Bible contains another episode of a mysterious divine figure who, after having wrestled all night with Jacob, refuses Jacob's request to learn his name, answering that he instead will give Jacob a new name, and from then on the patriarch will be called Israel. This is saying that man may not decide who God is, nor what God can and must do, but God can revolutionize the life of a man, giving him a new path and a new mission.

In the episode of the burning bush, in contrast to what happens to Jacob, God does tell his name to Moses, but it is an unpronounceable name, as though God wished to manifest himself and withdraw at the same moment. It is clear that God wishes to enter into a relationship with the people, but equally clear that they have no power over him. Whoever he might be, even as he reveals his name, this God insists forcefully on his own absolute liberty. And much more.[216]

Let's dwell for a moment on the name of God. The voice from the bush answers Moses's question, saying, "*'ehye asher 'ehye*,"; literally, "I am that I am." *'Ehye* is the verb *to be* in the imperfect tense, which indicates an action that is not terminated, complete, or is still underway in the present, past, and future. Since in Biblical Hebrew the verb is not conjugated to indicate *when* an act has been completed, but to express the *quality* of the action (that is, it does not refer to yesterday, today, or tomorrow, but says whether the actions was, is, or will be finite in itself, or rather whether it will continue), the phrase is to be read: *I* (the first person subject is normally understood rather than expressed); *asher*, meaning *who/that*, or can simply be translated with a colon, and once again *I am/I will be/I was*. The entire expression can take on a vast array of shadings and can be read as: *I am/will be he who/I am/I will be*; or: *I am/I will be who I will be*; or *I was who I am/will be. . .* And also: *I am here for you, I am what I was, I will be that which I have always been, I will be what I am, I was what I have been*, and so on.

After this, the voice specifies, *Thus shalt thou say unto the children of Israel, I am hath sent me unto you.* The abbreviated expression *'ehye*, which God uses when speaking of himself, becomes *haja* when he is spoken of. From all these meanings derives the proper name by which *this* God will be called from this moment on in the Bible, and is transcribed with the unpronounceable tetragrammaton *YHWH*.[217]

Scholars believe that in addition to the meanings associated with the being we are speaking of, the tetragrammaton also encompasses the root of the Arab word for love and that of an ecstatic cry that would mean, *Oh He!*[218] A few letters seem to enclose an almost inexhaustible richness of meaning, in which simplicity and infinity are inextricably interwoven! With the story of the burning bush, the redactor found a way to express a surprising intuition of divine essence. What idea of God comes from this?

First of all, this is a God who is absolutely free. His existence and essence depend solely on him: he exists only by his own will, and is what he wishes to be. Neither his nature nor his existence, and still less his manifestation depend on anything but his own freedom to choose. Luigi Pareyson observes that from this characteristic it becomes clear that freedom precedes creation, because the material reality of the world is rooted in the very being of God, in being *tout court* and, ultimately, in the freedom of being:

> Usually we think of the creation of the world as the supreme manifestation of divine liberty; but the freedom of God appears even before that at a much deeper level: at the root of his very being. . . God wants to exist and wants to be what he is, meaning that he is free not only with regard to being in general, but above all with regard to his own being. . . There is nothing more to say: it is an absolute act of will and freedom, with which God makes himself and declares himself master of his own being and of being in general.[219]

The root of the divine name includes the concept of existence: being means existing.[220] But the Hebrew mind and language are concrete and pragmatic, so that *being* means *being there.* The verb implies both a presence and a relationship. Thus *I am* means I exist, I am there, here and now and forever (as indicated by the imperfect tense) in relation with you, at your side, for you. The concept is that of an active presence, a divine involvement with the human and with history.

The entity speaking from the bush is not *existent* as an impersonal, indisputable first principal held by Greek philosophy to be at the origin of life. This being is different and more than that, with a surplus, so to speak, with respect to that Greek concept: this one not only *is* and *makes* being eternally; he is also eternally present and involved because he wishes to be so.[221] The God that Israel dares to imagine understands its condition (*the cry of the children of Israel is come unto me*) and he participates in its life because he is faithful to himself, to his irrevocable choices. The imperfect tense of the verb expresses the continuity and permanence of an action *in fieri*, and thus open to the future and to fulfillment. The name of God—and, since name and essence are identical, God himself—brings with it a promised future.

As we've said, however, the revealed name, extremely rich in meaning, remains unpronounceable. God remains ungraspable, escaping from any human attempt to compel him to serve private aims through magical practices that turn gods and the idols who represent them into instruments for the domination of other men and nature. This is yet another great liberating action: with the concept of the oneness, universality, freedom, and transcendence of the living God of the Jews, humanity liberates itself from magical thinking and the power of idols. The God encountered or conceived by Israel is not an idol, but *someone*; he is the reality of *being*. And has been observed, "You can say, 'I don't believe in God', but who can say, 'I don't believe in being?'"[222]

Abraham

Many generations before Moses, another character has an encounter, or an intuition, that will change his life and decisively influence the spiritual future of the West. The character is Abraham, a patriarch shared by the three monotheistic religions; his story is told in *Genesis*, the longest book in the Old Testament (50 chapters). Probably written after the return from Babylon between the VI and V century BCE, the first chapters recount the origins of the world and of human beings. They are elaborate cosmological myths, probably composed in polemic with the myths of other tribes in the region, with which the version of the Hebrews presents similarities but also important and substantial differences.[223]

The stories of the patriarchs of Israel begin at *Genesis* XII. They are Abraham, Isaac, and Jacob.

Already during the Babylonian exile, the Jews had felt a need to rethink and rewrite their histories to keep them from being forgotten or swallowed up by the highly developed and victorious culture of Mesopotamia. Those of the Hebrews who returned to their traditional homeland subsequent to an edict issued by Cyrus, King of the Persians, had to confront many problems, including the need to reconstruct or reconfirm a national identity that had been gravely compromised by the long years of exile. With this aim they collected and gathered into one place the many tales in circulation of the affairs and traditions of the various tribes of Israel. These were usually linked to precise geographical locations: the stories of Abraham's tribe centered on Hebron; stories of the tribe of Jacob were oriented around the city of Bethel; Joseph was associated with Dohan, north of Sichem. All these traditions were assembled into the unified history of a great family, that of the *children of Israel.*

The foundation of this huge task of collecting and reconceiving the diverse traditions into a single great history was the certainty, on the part of the Jews who returned to Jerusalem in 538 BCE to reconstruct their destroyed city, that the same God who had freed their ancestors from slavery in Egypt had also freed their descendants from slavery in Babylon. It was God's action that made it possible for them to return to their homeland. For these Jews, these separate stories were in truth a single history. What Israel wanted to declare before the whole world through the accounts in *Genesis* was the unquestionable superiority of their God over the gods of the Babylonians (and all other gods). Despite all the adversity, the scattering of the tribes, their weakness in the face of much more powerful enemies, their God had been so powerful as to lead them back to their own land.

But let's return to the story of Abraham. He was originally from Ur, an ancient Sumerian city in southern Mesopotamia near the source of the Tigris. Tradition holds that his father, Terach, had been a vendor of idols. Their entire tribe later moved to another city in the north of Mesopotamia, Harran, where Abraham's adventures began after the death of his father. The Bible tells that Abraham was already old, wealthy, and childless; that is, in the worst possible condition for a man of his era, when the lack of progeny was considered a divine curse. We can easily imagine him, thanks in part to many movies that have told the story, as he gazes out over the desert and reflects on the emptiness and sadness in his heart, asking what's the point of a life so long but so sterile. Suddenly, without the text's author having prepared readers for the change, a direct discourse begins: a voice sharply exhorts Abraham, "Get thee out of thy country, and from thy kindred, and from thy father's house, unto a land that I will shew thee." (Genesis 12,1).

The King James Bible translates with the exhortatory-imperative "Get thee out" the original Hebrew *lech lecha*, a typical and frequent biblical expression that repeats a root to reinforce its meaning. Literally this means something like *Get yourself going* but also *go to yourself, go in yourself*.[224] The voice that summons Abraham to leave urges him also to look fearlessly within himself, to understand himself and what he wants, and to begin something completely new even at the price of shredding his bonds with the tradition and religion of his fathers.

It is a strong invitation to discover a previously unrecognized internal and psychological liberty which will be seen to be central, many centuries later, to the teaching of Jesus of Nazareth and Paul of Tarsus.[225] This liberty undergirds the exercise of free will, the capacity to choose even in the face of one's cultural conditioning and social conformism.[226] It is asked of Abraham that he risk his life for an intuition.

Among all the old customs and certainties he must abandon by leaving his own land, his relatives, and the house of his father, the most gravid with consequences for the future is the cult of idols, which in that era was the key of all religion. The internal voice of the patriarch, speaking unexpectedly and far from the centers of history, told him that a living God existed, one not constructed by the hands of man. On the basis of this intuited faith handed down by Abraham to his descendants, the Jews have risked their existence, abandoning belief in tribal gods in favor of a single, living, universal God, the source of all life. This is the beginning of a continuous battle against any form of the idolatry that makes people slaves, an unending struggle never completely won.

Ever since Abraham, the forces of nature are no longer divine, but merely phenomena that arouse wonder and fear only because mankind is fragile and doesn't always know how to defend itself. Over time, this new way of comprehending nature will bring about the birth and development of scientific research.

The entire Bible is a story of liberation: from idols, from fear, from the precariousness of existence, and Abraham is the first to begin the long journey of progressive emancipation that will lead humankind beyond myth, to free itself from the seductions of magic. Mankind will become conscious of its own dignity and its own strength in a world freed from the fear of incomprehensible, supernatural powers. Abraham's courageous choice was made freely and generated freedom because he was not asked to submit and obey; instead he was offered an alliance. This is what makes his experience emblematic.

Eden

The first three chapters in *Genesis* recount the origins of the world, of life, of suffering and death. The first chapters present two different versions of creation, and scholars maintain that the second one is the oldest, while the first version furnishes a framing introduction. The stories include the creation of the world, the disobedience of Adam and Eve who, tempted by the serpent, eat the fruit of the forbidden tree, and their banishment from Eden. This assemblage of myths, as we've said, was intended to provide a specific cosmogony which is not dissimilar from others that were in circulation in Mesopotamia and the Middle East, but it stands apart for several substantial elements that make the biblical perception of the world quite different from its contemporaries.

First among these is the implicit centrality, recognized by many commentators although the term itself never appears, of freedom. The first two chapters dwell especially on divine freedom, while the successive chapters deal with human freedom.[227]

The language of the narration is typically mythopoetic, not offering historical events but the particular viewpoint of the narrating authors, meaning that in order to understand the text we must try to imagine what questions they were responding to. To do this we must immerse ourselves in the historical situation of Israel, having returned to Jerusalem after the Babylonian exile, with the conviction that it had already been twice freed from slavery, first in Egypt and then in Babylon. The essential fact is that in contrast to many others in the same circumstances, a small group of nomadic tribes, a people of little importance, had not been swallowed up by a far greater power!

What does Israel deduce from this fact in the context of the sensibilities of its era? It deduces that a God has protected and freed them. It is thus quite natural to ask who such a benevolent God might be, and what rapport such a God has not only with Israel but with the whole world. Numerous scholars think that the first three chapters of Genesis were composed to respond to questions of this type and to explain in retrospect, the conception of God that emerged from such experiences. This would also explain why, as is generally held, these stories came late in the intellectual development of Israel, during an advanced phase in its cultural evolution. When undertaking the final redaction of its sacred texts, the sages of the era probably also elaborated an overall religious-philosophical vision that took account of the knowledge available. It is reasonable to suppose they asked what such a powerful God must have done before manifesting himself to Israel, and what relation did he have with humanity and the world?

In a certain sense the sages must have returned to the idea handed down that this divine being must be *in the beginning* (*bereshit*), he must be at the origin of life and all things. They must have concluded that he must have been not only the creator of Israel, but of the Universe itself. Through these logical steps, Israel—in total contrast to the world around it at that time—came to conceive the idea of a single, universal God.[228]

In the beginning, or *before all*, according to the translation that some hold to be etymologically closer to the Hebrew *bereshit*, there is only *Elohim*, the divine plurality, which creates by pronouncing a word, usually rendered in English as *Let there be*.[229] At the beginning of all, before and above everything else, there is being. And then immediately, summoned by his word, comes light (incidentally, it's curious to note that already in the Vth century BCE, people intuit that light—photons—are the beginning of the material world). Alongside light shadow is also born, and shadows do not have a different nature; instead they are simply the absence of light, its negation or rejection. The dynamic is similar to the way the affirmation of being entails the alternative possibility of the negation of being, which emerges as a product of existence itself.

After having created light, God orders the elements, separating light from darkness and the waters of the sky from those of the Earth.

It is interesting to note that *Genesis* does not speak of creation from *nothingness*, a concept that does not exist in Semitic mentality, but of *separation*. The verb is *barà*, translated into English as *he created*, which makes sense, but the original meaning pertains to *separating out* rather than to *forging* something from nothing. God gives shape to the world by ordering chaotic matter (before God's action, the world was *tohu we bohu*, obscure words that indicate disorder and obscurity), that chaos which is closest to the idea of nothingness in Semitic languages. Before all this, there was only the *ruah* of Elohim: the *spirit* or the *powerful wind* of God. Biblical scholar Daniel Attinger makes note that in the beginning there is not nothing, not *nothingness*, but neither is there life. There is only the void and a powerful wind. Pointing out that the word *berit*, alliance, derives from the word *barà*, André Chouraqui asserts that "creation fundamentally constitutes an act of alliance."[230] In the biblical context, creation is the result and sign of an alliance between God, the source of being, and God's most precious fruit, life.

If there is a beginning, there is also a *before*. In *Genesis* creation is not the beginning, but the consequence of something that took place earlier, an *event in the life of God*—and this is the *before* of creation—from which all else derives. From a decision of divine freedom concerning itself there emanates a second decision, the choice in favor of life, our *bereschit*.

The biblical vision of creation expresses the idea that the world, from the Universe to microbes, is caused neither by necessity nor by chance, but as the outcome of a positive will. The existence of the world expresses someone's freedom, and the world itself bears the sign of the positivity, the benevolence that willed it or at least desired life. At its root, so to speak, there is a surplus value of goodness.

Before all, then, there is the unfathomable mystery of God hidden behind the small, initial *bet*, open to the future and closed toward the past. That is to say that the story of God before us, his original life, concerns only him and his freedom. The biblical God wishes to reveal himself only through his actions, at least until the appearance of the Nazarene. In the second chapter of *Genesis*, the cosmos and the ordering action of God are no longer at the center of the narration; instead, it is the creation of the human, human liberty and its first consequences. The first man is Adam, the creature of Earth, from whom will be drawn a creature equal to and different from him, who can stand up to him. Diverse exegetes point out that Adam recognizes himself as human, as *ish*, rather than solely *adam* (terrestrial), only in the moment when he sees this new creature. Addressing her he calls her *isha*, the feminine form of *ish*, which we translate as woman, but would more appropriately be translated by giving a feminine ending to the noun *human*. Man and woman recognize each other reciprocally in their different identities only by encountering one another and looking into one another's eyes.

The story continues with the prohibition that the two must observe not to eat the fruit of the tree standing in the center of the garden, while they may eat of every other plant. More precisely, they are told there are two trees in the center of the garden. One is the Tree of Life, a figure widely disseminated in many Sumerian and Babylonian mythologies. The other is the Tree of the Knowledge of Good and Evil, which appears only in *Genesis*, and is thus unique to Israel. This is the tree of the forbidden fruit.

In this prohibition, many have long chosen to read an implicit condemnation of human freedom, with the consequence that they have imputed to the biblical God a malevolent wish to keep human beings in a condition of intellectual inferiority, ignorant and thus incapable of making choices. In truth, however, this myth expresses something very different. What is prohibited is the human pretense to decide for itself what is good and what is evil. These values, in fact, have been established by the same source from which being has poured forth, which precedes and transcends mankind. Nature and the qualities of good and evil derive from the origin of being, not from the decision of mankind, since he is himself an effect of the same cause from which all things come.

Within the limits of its own nature, human freedom is no different from the originary freedom, because there are not different types of freedom, but only different expressions or gradations of the one freedom. Thus the human being may even disobey God and decide on his or her own to commit good or evil. Mankind therefore is not innocent, because it can choose, knowing what it is doing. Freedom itself excludes innocence, which after all, as Pareyson says, has no moral merit, but the choice to do good does. This is what the Tree of Knowledge symbolizes: the need to know in order to have moral merit, and thus to choose the good.

The existence of evil precedes that of mankind, just as the tree exists before the existence of *Adam*. The responsibility for evil cannot rest entirely on the shoulders of man, but he is free to decide whether to *take* and *eat* the apple, which means, metaphors aside, that he has the power to translate evil into reality with his actions.

This tree, so perilous and fundamental—located at the very center of Eden—that symbolizes consciousness, without which there would be neither freedom of choice (free will) nor responsibility, is left unguarded. There are no fences or guardian angels to keep the first couple from transgressing and eating its fruit.[231] This means that their freedom is not false, but so real that they can do whatever they want, even to the point of ignoring the will of the garden's owner.

Why did God allow them to do it? If the fruit was so dangerous, why didn't he stop them from eating it? Perhaps the author's intention was to find an explanation for how death could be compatible with the existence of a good God, so the author made mankind guilty of disobedience. To leave mankind a whisper of hope, however, the redactor alleviated the responsibility with the intervention of an evil creature represented as a serpent. That's one possible explanation.

I think we can look at the matter from another viewpoint, interpreting this myth from a more philosophical-metaphysical than religious perspective, to suggest another answer to the question.

The fact that nothing but their own will can keep Adam and Eve from eating that fruit seems to me to indicate symbolically that nothing, absolutely nothing—not even rejecting God, destroying Eden, and introducing death itself into the order of life—is so evil as to justify the elimination of liberty from the realm of existence. If this is so—and this is the question that ultimately inspired this lengthy reflection—I think it is natural to ask why freedom is so indispensable. The answer may be found in Pareyson's intuition, where we started out. Even if we will never succeed in fully understanding it, freedom has given and gives reality its structure, its evolutionary and unfolding vitality. Freedom is the energy from which existence originates, something we can imagine as the DNA of being, its intrinsic dynamic. Thus it was and will always be indispensable, ineradicable, and inevitable, at least as long as the Universe subsists.

And perhaps even after.

Conclusions

To Recapitulate

The first objective I set for myself when undertaking this research was to verify as much as possible Luigi Pareyson's hypothesis that identified freedom as such an important structural element of reality that the existence of one would be impossible without the other.

The first necessary condition, therefore, was that liberty be found in action in the dynamics of the physical and biological evolution of the world (by which word we mean all that exists). Only under this condition could it be said that freedom is not only a matter of human beings, but precedes them and in some way exists in and of itself.

To ascertain how things stand, we have together taken a voyage of not many pages, but they have been intense and rather complex, leading us into diverse and difficult disciplines. It would be well, then, to gather the threads of the discourse by repeating the principal points we have touched on, beginning with Pareyson's hypothesis. We will next summarize what we have discovered about the action of freedom in the cosmos, in matter, and in biological life, and what interpretation of reality results from our exploration. Lastly, we shall offer a few conclusions.

1.   Philosophy is born from the question: *why does something exist rather than nothing?*

According to our hypothesis, the answer is that being exists as the result of a choice in its favor, that is as an *act* of absolute freedom which wanted something to exist rather than nothing. All that exists is not the outcome of some form of unavoidable *necessity*; on the contrary, it might just as easily never have existed.

Among the consequences that derive from this hypothesis, the first is the absolutely precarious character of existence in all its manifestations. It is as though everything found itself surrounded by nothingness, suspended over an abyss into which it could fall at any moment (remember the Higgs boson). This disconcerting situation, if considered rightly, can arouse contradictory sensations. On one hand, dwelling on the absence of a firm foundation, on the lack of a *mathematical* certainty that guarantees the continuance of existence—even without me or us and despite the errors we commit as a species—is rather anguishing. But looking at things from another point of view, we can feel ourselves to be tremendously fortunate, knowing that nothing made our presence a sure thing, that the Universe itself might not exist at all or might not count us among its inhabitants. The absolute gratuitousness of our existence amazes us, provoking gratitude. This antinomy is the first of many we have encountered in these pages.

2.   Ambiguity pertains to liberty intrinsically, almost a symptom of it, that marks the world and reappears at every level. Where does it come from, and why?

To answer, we have to begin with the *nature* of nothingness. Nothingness does not precede being; it is not a void in which something suddenly manifests itself. Rather, it arises together with being, simultaneously, out of that single initial force that is freedom. The same dynamic gives life to being, because in the very moment being is chosen, the contrary alternative becomes possible. Being and nothingness—opposites to the maximum degree—are connatural in the originary freedom, making it thus ambiguous, potentially open to both. The choice in favor of being, however, has rendered nothingness a discarded potentiality.

The ambiguity of nature appears especially clearly in the human condition for diverse reasons. First of all, because by being born we enter an already existent world, which is thus both the very condition of our freedom and its most enclosing limit. Second of all, due to the fact that we cannot avoid being free. We are obligated to make choices, because even in *refusing* to choose we would be making a choice, thus exercising our freedom. Last of all, because it is liberty that makes us able to do either good or evil, and this is its most dramatic aspect, which has imprinted our existence with perilous ambiguity, rendering it "the heart of reality [. . .] tragic and aching."[232]

3.   The question of evil is ontological before it is ethical or moral. What is evil and where does it come from?

For an answer we must again start from the same point, the moment when freedom chose being—which by virtue of this choice became *good*—establishing as *evil* the not-chosen alternative (not being). Then began the dialectic between being and nothingness, between good and evil. There is no original perfection from which decay somehow set in, and we have never been in an earthly paradise from which we were banished for having committed an unpardonable sin. It is true that there has always been and always will be for every person in every moment of life the alternative, *temptation*. Even God, the originary, absolute freedom, in the beginning chose and defeated a *temptation* that was his alone: the temptation to remain in himself. This is the ontological root of evil: the *temptation of nothingness*, the alternative rejected by God, which mankind's choices transform into *active* evil, suffering inflected, pure pain. We are not the origin of evil because we did not introduce it into the world. It exists from the beginning, well before our appearance, and we have the power to transform it into gesture and action. This removes a useless burden from our shoulders, but leaves intact all the weight of our responsibilities.

4.   Because it is so contradictory, the world can be perceived in two ways: "in its gratuitousness or in its unfoundedness."[233]

The positive and reassuring thought of its gratuitousness locates us in a Universe we can imagine as sustained by unbounded, generous, and loving liberality. But the idea of having no other foundation for our existence than the freedom of a *will* that we cannot in any way condition, and that we can only hope continues to sustain us, leads us back to precariousness and uncertainty. The human situation is such that we can believe ourselves cradled in the hand of an infinite, irrevocable, and powerful benevolence, or to be the fragile and finally insignificant result of the indifferent dynamics of a process that could be interrupted at any moment. Every option is possible, and each person has their own good explanation, but none can be proven irrefutably. Even in the interpretation we impose on the world and our lives we find ourselves completely free to choose the reading we prefer.

5.   Moving to a consideration of the physical world, it soon becomes apparent that incompleteness, alternatives, and mistakes are indispensable to progress, evolution, and life.

This means that the Universe creates itself thanks to a dynamic of freedom, in an openness to diverse possibilities. It begins in a *disturbance* that ruptures the stasis of perfect symmetry and creates a movement in which different possible events can take place.[234] From its first instant, the Universe is born endowed with freedom (which John Polkinghorne calls *freedom of process*) and the laws of nature are the expression of a specific freedom of matter.[235] At this level too, the dynamic of the physical world is a weaving of liberty and necessity, of interaction between universal constants and the unpredictable. Newtonian physics can perfectly explain the laws of the world we live in, while indeterminacy dominates in the subatomic world, that of the essential substance of matter.

One of the most interesting aspects of this dynamic is the fact that quantum physics not only overturns the determinism that governs other dimensions of reality, but also the traditional and *simple* distinctions between the physical and the metaphysical. The particles that compose reality can have a double nature: they move from one place to another by jumping over the intermediate points and virtually do not exist during the leap. They have no individuality because they are indistinguishable one from another no matter where they are. Like photons, they do not age; like neutrinos, they penetrate solid bodies, and once in contact, they remain in relation with one another no matter where they stray in the Universe (the phenomenon known as *entanglement*).

Carlo Rovelli claims that quantum physics have revealed three fundamental aspects of reality: its *granularity*, which means that there is a limit, represented by Planck's constant, "to the information that can exist in a system"; *indeterminism*, which means that the future cannot be predicted; its *relation*, the fact that events are interactive. "The world of existing things is reduced to the world of possible interactions. Reality comes down to interaction; reality is reduced to relation."[236] In sum, "the plot of the world comes not from objects but from the relations among them and their processes."[237] The indubitable philosophical import of this assertion represents a good example of the way the discoveries of quantum physics, revolutionizing our vision of the material world, have given new vigor and drive to philosophical and metaphysical speculation as well.[238]

6.   Observing biological life, we see from its most elemental process—metabolism—that it displays a kernel of freedom in the way an organism maintains its own form while transforming the substance it feeds on (in contrast to inorganic matter, which can change form but always conserves its own substance). At the same time, however, a kernel of necessity is also already present in the metabolic process since an organism *must transform* matter in order to live; otherwise it

would die. Lastly, even from its most elementary expression, the organism has a purpose: it wants to live.

Relation and indeterminacy present themselves to the maximum degree in the biological world. Biological life manifests itself as relation in the collaboration among cells to permit the organism to live and evolve, whereas disaggregation leads to death. The history of the evolution of species clearly demonstrates that nothing is determined *a priori* and that the future is impossible to predict, because there is never a single possible future, as demonstrated by the Cambrian decimation. We may never have arrived exactly where we find ourselves today, and might not have come to be at all.

Last, it's important to stress the fundamental role played by error in the evolution of living things, because error is possible only when there is freedom. Perfection such as perfect symmetry is sterile, while mistakes are fertile. If imperfections had never been produced, the world today would probably be populated only by bacteria. Errors in copying DNA lead to progress in species, just as they produce disease and deformity.

7.   After have reconstructed in summary form the identity of the world's reality, we move on to its interpretation. We are compelled to ask whether so much miraculous development has a purpose, and what that purpose might reasonably be. This is not merely a psychological desire, although such a desire is entirely legitimate, since psychology teaches us that finding a purpose in our experience is fundamental to mental equilibrium and individual contentment.

At the root of the striving for purpose, however, is the desire to grasp a truth that allows a glimpse of itself, only to conceal itself again like a capricious beauty, either too timid or aware of the shattering effect the full vision of it would provoke. The infinite exploration is for a meaning in the whole cosmic adventure. True, some insist that the Universe has no meaning, but it is equally true that it has somehow produced intelligent rational beings who ask a vast multitude of questions, to which many answers have been found. Do we find ourselves in the paradox of a meaningless *totality* within which a species composed of fragments of reality has developed an innate need to learn the meaning of everything? How can the very idea that there is a meaning in things come to be?

Among the diverse opinions we discussed in Chapter Four, the idea that there is an intelligent mind at the origin of the Universe has revealed itself to be the only one capable of including all the factors from whose unfolding action the reality we know takes shape: chance, necessity, contingency, and freedom. This is the only idea that affirms the overall comprehensibility of the process while maintaining unpredictability in the outcome.

As to the question, newly rendered urgent by quantum physics, of whether the ultimate nature of reality is material or spiritual, one stimulating hypothesis is Vito Mancuso's proposal of considering reality as *dual*; that is, a single substance that manifests itself in two modes, a single energy that is both force and matter. Equally interesting is his interpretation of biological evolution as a process with a goal, but without either a pre-established course or an endpoint guaranteed by *necessity*.

Personally, I do not fully subscribe to the idea that, "the only plausible meaning of the existence of the world is the birth of freedom which fulfills itself in love."[239] I would hold, along with Pareyson, that freedom precedes the existence of the world, and believe that love motivated the originary freedom to act.

I believe that the mysterious singularity that sparked the world and brought to flame the generative freedom of life must be love itself. Everything that exists can be explained according to something that precedes it. Even freedom, understood as creative force, must be motivated by something, by a reason that urges it to manifest itself precisely in that *moment* and in the *act* that it decides to perform. This something does not precede it because nothing precedes the beginning, but belongs to it and is connatural with it. I think this thing may be love, which by definition is gratuitous (it has no need of an external motivation to reveal itself) and is the only reality that finds solely within itself its own justification. Love may have motivated freedom to act, may have compelled *God* to come out of himself to give life to the Universe and all that it contains. As Pareyson says, ". . . perhaps we can say that God so wants the creation of the world that to make it happen he wills himself into existence."[240]

I imagine love the same way science imagines that originary power—hypothesized but not yet identified experimentally—from which the four fundamental forces of nature burst forth. Mysterious, fecund, rationally possible, I imagine it as the will that willed itself with an act of unlimited, unrestrainable freedom. Lastly (and why shouldn't I?), I also imagine it as the divine word which, in being pronounced, gives life to the world.

8.   The expression *divine word* brings us to the Bible, the pre-eminent foundational text of western culture, an interpretation of the world and a vision of mankind deeply rooted in the idea of liberty. In biblical thought, the origin of exis-

tence derives from the freedom of a "living God, lover of life," who in the act of creation transmits something of himself into his creation. What he transmits, in fact, is his freedom, which finds in the human being its highest expression in all nature. The whole Bible recounts the dialogue, the encounter and clash between divine and human freedom. This dialectic offers a possible explanation of the apparently irreconcilable contradiction between the existence of an omnipotent, radically beneficent God and the obvious presence of evil on Earth, the central problem of theodicy and principal objection of those who contest the faith that God exists.

Where does the biblical God stand with regard to evil? We have discussed this in part earlier in this chapter: God shores up and guarantees the defense of life against the ontological evil of nothingness. Concretely, however, why doesn't God keep mankind from committing evil? Why doesn't God impose the good? After all, wouldn't it be better if it was impossible for humans to perform evil actions? God's attitude toward the evil we commit is to submit to it. This concept should be particularly understandable to Christians, given the testimony of the life and death of Jesus of Nazareth. Why does God do this?

The first, obvious but non entirely satisfying answer is because God respects human liberty. But history has witnessed so much and such terrible horror and suffering that perhaps freedom isn't worth the price. Perhaps we have had and still have in our hands a tool we are incapable of handling, as Dostoevksy's Grand Inquisitor charged in the Introduction to this book.

There is a second possible answer, and that is that an imposed good is worse than evil, because love is impossible without freedom. Love is activated by freedom just the way particles activate the essential forces. To impose good would be a double evil, because it would mean simultaneously blocking freedom and love.

There is also, finally, a third answer, which seems to me to offer the best solution, and it has to do with the very nature of freedom. We have repeated that being and liberty are inseparable, and we have also posited that *God* is freedom, in the sense that liberty pertains intrinsically to God's nature. Ontologically, freedom must by definition be absolute, and conditioning or negating it would be to condition or negate the very possibility of being. From God's viewpoint, to impose good or interdict evil (the two are the same) would mean negating and contradicting himself, since God *is* freedom. To prohibit freedom to mankind, no matter what the consequences, would mean denying mankind's existence, because it would correspond to negating or impeding being, preferring nothingness. Thus God can only oppose, with his liberty, the consequences of human liberty, even when this freedom turns to evil.

In this way the originary, divine freedom, which irrevocably chose the world and life, offers itself up to our freedom only as the possibility of hope against the meaninglessness of the world and domination by evil.

In conclusion

> Quantum mechanics . . . today offers a spectacularly effective description of nature. The world is not madeup of fields and particles, but of a single type of entity: the quantum field. There are no longer particles that move in space with the passage of time, but quantum fields whose elementary events exist in spacetime. The world is strange but simple.[241]

This is how the Universe, including ourselves and our history, appears to us in light of the hypothesis that freedom constitutes its fundamental dynamic: a bit strange, no doubt, but not too complicated, and in sum not incomprehensible. Like all theories, this one too depends on reason, naturally, but also on imagination, and begins with the sort of postulate that is, "indispensable for any plan of research. To look for something, you have to suppose at the outset that what you seek can be explained."[242] Have we succeeded? I don't know, but I hope we have at least established a foundation that might spark someone's desire to keep on searching.

Returning to the first of Roberta De Monticelli's questions posed in the Introduction—whether freedom is something with a foundation in reality—I think we have collected sufficient evidence to answer affirmatively. There is no doubt that freedom belongs to the mechanisms at work in the biological and physical world, and thus it exists in the real world with or without our human selves, although we may be, here and now on Earth, the biological entities that express freedom to the maximum degree.

In answer to the second question—what does freedom attest to the existence of?—I would say that it depends on the overall interpretation we give to existence, with all its complementary factors. I have personally come to the conclusion that freedom attests to the existence of love as the primary impulse behind liberty itself, as *loving intelligence*: the eternal choice of goodness, the irrevocable *yes* to life, the meaning and goal of the entire adventure of all living creation. Like freedom, love too is transcendent and immanent, a reality

undefinable and yet known by all through its effects. We can compare it metaphorically to the dark energy that fills the Universe and that we know to exist,
without knowing what it is, through the effects it has on everything the Universe
contains.

The existence of freedom tells us that, yes, we are suspended over nothingness, but we can be held firmly by the hand of God, whoever that might be,
and it permits us to believe that our existence, although completely *useless*, is
appreciated and *welcomed* (literally, wanted by goodness and has come from
goodness). Our existence can be the realized desire of a love as powerful as the
freedom that expressed it. Freedom ultimately allows us to conceive of love not
as a feeling, but as a force that could be the foundation and guarantee of life.

In this book we've cited three different ways of recounting a beginning
that we still can't explain. Everyone talks about a movement, a rupture, a change
in form, from which something arises that had never been before, and which,
through an infinite series of events, has led to us. A disturbance in the metaphysical void, in the Universe or the heart of God. This is the limit where science, for
now, has stopped, awaiting the discovery of a new piece in the puzzle. Philosophy and religion, on the other hand, cannot stop to wait because their function is
to seek to make sense of the knowledge that has been acquired. The anxiety to
explain life and its mystery allows no respite to the human spirit. It is as though
in every person the words spoken to Adam and Abraham continued to resonate:
human, where are you? Go into yourself, discover who you are. Thinking of life
as a fabric whose weave is freedom and whose weft is love puts us in the condition Dietrich Bonhoeffer describes in a poem written as he awaited execution:
"By gentle powers lovingly surrounded /with patience we'll endure, let come
what may."[243]

Bibliography

1. AA.VV. (2003), *Dizionario di Spiritualità Biblico-Patristica, Libertà e liberazione nella Bibbia*, Rome, Borla.
2. ACZEL, A. D. (2014), *Perché la scienza non nega Dio*, Tr. it, Milan, Raffaello Cortina Editore, 2015.
3. ACZEL, A. D., *Why Science Does not Disprove God*, New York, Morrow, 2014.
4. ARENDT, H. (1954-1961), *Tra passato e futuro*, Tr. it. Milan, Garzanti, 1991.
5. ARENDT, H., *Between Past and Future*, London, Penguin, 2006.
6. ATTINGER, D. (2015), *Un Dio che si implica nella nostra storia: una lettura del libro della Genesi*, Magnanon, Corsi Biblici della Comunità di Bose, Edizioni Qiqajon, Comunità di Bose, version in pdf.
7. AYALA, F. J. (2007), *Il dono di Darwin alla scienza e alla religione*, Tr. it. Milan, Edizioni San Paolo, 2009.
8. AYALA, F. J., *Darwin's Gift to Science and Religion*, Washington DC, Joseph Henry Press, 2007.
9. AYALA, F.J. (2012), *Evoluzione*, Tr. it. Bari, Edizioni Dedalo.
10. AYALA, F.J., *Evolution, Explanation, Ethics and Aesthetics: Towards a Philosophy of Biology*, Cambridge MA, Academic Press, 2016
11. BALBI, A. (2016), *Dove sono tutti quanti?* Milan, Rizzoli.
12. BERDJAEV, N. (1927), *Filosofia dello spirito libero*, Tr. it. Milan, San Paolo, 1997.
13. BERDJAEV, N. *Freedom and the Spirit*, Brooklyn, Semantron Press, 2009
14. BOCCHI, G. CERUTI, M. (1993), *Origini di storie*, Milan, Feltrinelli.
15. BONCINELLI, E. OFFEDDU, L. (2005), *Prodigi quotidiani*, Milan, Boroli Editore.
16. BONCINELLI, E. (2014), *Alla ricerca delle leggi di Dio*, Milan, Rizzoli.
17. BONHOEFFER, D. (1944), *Poesie*, Magnano, Edizioni Qiqajon, Comunità di Bose, 1999.
18. BONHOEFFER, D., *Dietrich Bonhoeffer's Prison Poems*, ed. and trans. Edward Robertson, Zondervan, 2005.
19. BOVATI, P. (2012), *Parole di libertà*, Milan,EDB, 2008.
20. BRYSON, B., *A Short History of Nearly Everything*, New York, Broadway Books, 2003.

21. CAPRA, F. LUISI, P.L. (2014), *Vita e natura. Una visione sistemica*, Tr. it. Sansepolcro, Aboca.
22. CAPRA, F. LUISI, P.L, *The Systems View of Life: A Unifying Vision*, Cambridge, Cambridge University Press, 2016.
23. CAVALLI SFORZA, L.L. PIEVANI, T. (2011), *Homo sapiens. La grande storia della diversità umana* (catalogo della mostra Palazzo delle Esposizioni Roma), Turin, Codice Edizioni.
24. CAVALLI SFORZA, L.L., *The Great Human Diasporas: The History of Diversity and Evolution*, New York, Perseus Books, 1996.
25. CHIABERGE, R. (2008), *La variabile Dio. In cosa credono gli scienziati? Un confronto tra George Coyne e Arno Penzias*, Milan, Longanesi.
26. CHOURAQUI, A. (2001), *Il mio testamento. Il fuoco dell'alleanza*, Tr. it. Brescia, Queriniana, B2002.
27. CIANCI, C. (2012), *Percorsi della libertà*, Milan-Udine, Mimesis Edizioni.
28. DALL'AGLIO MARAMOTTI, M. (2007), *I legami della libertà*, Bologna, il Mulino.
29. DAVIES, P. (1983), *God and the New Physics*, New York, Simon and Schuster, 1983.
30. DE DUVE, C. (2002), *Come evolve la vita*, Tr. it. Milan, Raffaello Cortina Editore, 2003.
31. DE DUVE, C, *Life Evolving: Molecules, Mind, and Meaning*, London, Oxford University Press, 2002.
32. DE DUVE, C. (2009), *Genetica del peccato originale. Il peso del passato sul futuro della vita*, Tr. it. Milan, Raffaello Cortina Editore, 2010.
33. DE DUVE, C., *Genetics of Original Sin: The Impact of Natural Selection on the Future of Humanity*, New Haven, Yale Universiry Press, 2012.
34. DE DUVE, C. (2011), *Da Gesù a Gesù passando per Darwin*, Tr. it. Milan, Edizioni San Paolo, 2013.,
35. DE MONTICELLI, R. (2009), *La novità di ognuno*, Milan, Garzanti, 2012.
36. DE WAAL, F. (2016), *Siamo così intelligenti da capire l'intelligenza degli altri animali?*, Milan, Raffaello Cortina Editore.
37. DE WAAL, F., *The Age of Empathy: Nature's Lessons for a Kinder Society*, London, Souvenir Press, 2010.
38. DENNETT, D.C. (2003), *L'evoluzione della libertà*, Tr. it. Milan, Raffaello Cortina Editore, 2004.
39. DENNETT, D.C., *Consciousness Explained*, New York, Back Bay Books, 1992.
40. DI SANTE, C. (2012), *Dio e i suoi volti*, Milan, Edizioni San Paolo.
41. DORATO, M. (2007), *Cosa c'entra l'anima con gli atomi?* Bari, Laterza, 2007.
42. D'ORMESSON, J. (2010), *Che cosa strana è il mondo*, Tr. it. Florence, Barbès Editore, 2011.
43. D'ORMESSON, J. (2013), *Un giorno me ne andrò senza aver detto tutto*, Tr. it. Florence, Edizioni Clichy, 2014.
44. DOSTOEVSKY, *The Brothers Karamazov*, trans. Pevear & Volokhonsky, New York, Farar, Straus & Giroux, 2002.

45.   DYSON, F. (1979), *Turbare l'universo*, Tr. it. Turin, Bollati Boringhieri, 1999.
46.   DYSON, F. (1979), *Disturbing the Universe*, New York, Harper & Row, 1979.
47.   FEYNMAN, M. (2016), *Le battute memorabili di Feynman*, Tr. it. Milan, Adelphi 2017.
48.   FEYNMAN, M., *The Quotable Feynman*, Princeton, Princeton University Press, 2015.
49.   FLEW, A. (con VARGHESE, R.A.) (2007), *Dio esiste. Come l'ateo più famoso del mondo ha cambiato idea*, Tr. it. Caltanisetta, Alfa&Omega, 2010.
50.   FLEW, A., *There is a God: How the World's Most Notorious Atheist Changed His Mind*, New York, Harper One, 2008.
51.   FRANKL, V. (1969), *Senso e valori per l'esistenza*, Rome, Città Nuova, 1994.
52.   FRANKL, V. (1984), *Homo patiens*, Tr. it. Brescia, Queriniana, 1998.
53.   FRANKL, V., *Man's Search for Meaning*, Boston, Beacon Press, 2006.
54.   GALFARD, C. (2015), *L'universo a portata di mano*, Tr. it. Turin, Bollati Boringhieri, 2016.
55.   GALFARD, C., *Universe in your Hand*, New York, Flatiron Books, 2017.
56.   GAZZANIGA, M.S. (2008), *Human. Quel che ci rende unici*, Tr. it. Milan, Raffaello Cortina Editore, 2009.
57.   GAZZANIGA, M.S., *Human. The Science Behind What Makes Your Brain Unique*, New York, Harper Perennial, 2009.
58.   GIORELLO, G. SINDONI E. (2016), *Un mondo di mondi*, Milan, Raffaello Cortina Editore.
59.   GOULD, S. J. (1989), *La vita meravigliosa*, Milan, Feltrinelli, 1995.
60.   GOULD, S. J. (1989) *Wonderful Life. The Burgess Shale and the Nature of History*, New York, W. W. Norton, 1989.
61.   GRIBBIN, J. (1998), *Dizionario enciclopedico di fisica quantistica*, Tr. it. Cesena, Macro Edizioni, 2004.
62.   HAWKING, S.W. (2001), *L'universo in un guscio di noce*, Milan, Mondadori, 2006.
63.   HAWKING, S.W. (2005), *La grande storia del tempo*, Milan, BUR, 2015.
64.   HAWKING, S.W. (2010), *Il grande disegno*, Milan, Mondadori, 2012.
65.   HAWKING, S.W., *The Grand Design*, New York, Bantam 2010.
66.   HENDEL, R. (2013), *Il libro della Genesi*, Tr. it. Bologna, il Mulino, 2017.
67.   HENDEL, R., *The Book of Genesis: A Biography*, Princeton, Princeton University Press, 2012.
68.   HESCHEL, A.J. (1951), *Il sabato*, Tr. it. Garzanti, Milano 1999.
69.   HESCHEL, A.J. (1951), *The Sabbath. Its Meaning for Modern Man*, New York, Farrar Straus & Giroux, 1951.
70.   HESCHEL, A.J. (1962), *Il messaggio dei profeti*, Rome, Edizioni Borla, 1993.
71.   HESCHEL, A.J., *The Prophets*, New York, Harper Perennial, 2001.
72.   HESCHEL, A.J. (1966), *Il canto della libertà*, Magnano, Edizioni Qiqajon, Comunità di Bose, 1999.
73.   HESCHEL, A.J. (1990), *Crescere in saggezza*, Milan, Gribaudi, 2001.

74.   HOFFMANN, P. (2012), *Gli ingranaggi di Dio. Dal caos molecolare alla vita*, Tr. it. Turin, Bollati Boringhieri, 2014.
75.   JASPERS, K. (1948), *La fede filosofica*, Tr. it. Milan, Raffaello Cortina Editore, 2005.
76.   JONAS, H. (1979), *Il principio responsabilità. Un'etica per la civiltà tecnologica*, Tr. it. Turin, Einaudi, 2002.
77.   JONAS, H., *The Imperative of Responsibility: In Search of an Ethic for the Technological Age*, Chicago, University of Chicago Press, 1986.
78.   JONAS, H. (1987), *Il concetto di Dio dopo Auschwitz*, Tr. it. Genova, il melangolo, 1993.
79.   JONAS, H. (1993), *Sull'orlo dell'abisso. Conversazioni sul rapporto tra uomo e natura*, Tr. it. Turin, Einaudi, 2000.
80.   JONAS, H. (1994), *Organismo e libertà. Verso una biologia filosofica*, Tr. it. Turin, Einaudi, 1999.
81.   JOU, D. (2008), *Riscrivere la Genesi*, Tr. it. Rome, Castelvecchi, (2009) 2014.
82.   LEDOUX, J. (2015), *Ansia*, Tr. it. Milan, Raffaello Cortina Editore, 2016.
83.   LEDOUX, J., *Anxious. Using the Brain to Understand and Treat Fear and Anxiety*, New York, Penguin, 2016.
84.   LESCH, A. (2003), *Fisica da tasca*, Tr. it. Milan, Ponte alle Grazie, 2007.
85.   LÉVINAS, E. (1976), *Difficile libertà*, Tr. it. Brescia, La Scuola, 2000.
86.   LÉVINAS, E., *Difficult Freedom: Essays on Judaism*, Baltimore, Johns Hopkins University Press, 1997.
87.   LÉVINAS, E. (1982), *L'aldilà del versetto*, Tr.it. Napoli, Guida, 1986.
88.   LOMBARDINI, P. (2011), *Cuore di Dio, cuore dell'uomo*, Bologna, EDB.
89.   MANCUSO, V. (2011), *Io e Dio*, Milan, Garzanti.
90.   MANCUSO, V. (2013), *Il principio passione*, Milan, Garzanti.
91.   MANZI, G. (2006), *Homo sapiens*, Bologna, il Mulino.
92.   MANZI, G. (2007), *L'evoluzione umana*, Bologna, il Mulino.
93.   MANZI, G. (2013), *Il grande racconto dell'evoluzione umana*, Bologna, il Mulino.
94.   MARTINI, C.M. (1999), *Orizzonti e limiti della scienza. Decima cattedra dei non credenti*, Milan, Raffaello Cortina Editore.
95.   MCGRATH, A. (2015), *La grande domanda*, Tr. it. Turin, Bollati Boringheri, 2016.
96.   MCGRATH, A., *Born to Wonder: Exploring our Deepest Questions – Why are We Here and Why Does It Matter?*, Carol Stream, IL, Tyndale Momentum, 2020.
97.   MONOD, J. (1970), *Il caso e la necessità. Saggio sulla filosofia naturale della biologia contemporanea*, Tr. it. Mondadori, Milano 1971.
98.   NAGEL, T. (1974), *Cosa si prova a essere un pipistrello?* Tr. it. Castelvecchi, Roma 2013.
99.   NAGEL, T. (1987), *Una brevissima introduzione alla filosofia*, Tr. it. il Saggiatore, Milano 2014.
100. NATOLI, S. (1986), *L'esperienza del dolore*, Feltrinelli, Milano.
101. NATOLI, S. (2002), *Libertà e destino nella tragedia greca*, Morcelliana, Brescia.

102. NATOLI, S. (2008), *Edipo e Giobbe. Contraddizione e paradosso*, Morcelliana, Brescia.
103. NATOLI, S. (2016), *Il rischio di fidarsi*, il Mulino, Bologna.
104. OVADIA, M. (2002), *Vai a te stesso*, Einaudi, Torino.
105. PAREYSON, L. (1995), *Ontologia della libertà*, Einaudi, Torino 2000.
106. PAREYSON, L. (1998), *Essere Libertà Ambiguità*, Mursia, Milano.
107. PAREYSON, L., *Existence, Interpretation, Freedom. Selected Writings*, ed. by Paolo Diego Bubbio, trans. by Silvia Benso, Aurora CO, The Davies Group Publishers, 2009.
108. PAREYSON, L. (2011), *Persona e libertà*, (a cura di G. Riconda), LaScuola, Brescia.
109. PAREYSON, L., *Truth and Interpretation*, ed. by Silvia Benso, trans. by Robert T. Valgenti, New York, SUNY Press, 2014.
110. PARIS, L. (2012), *Sulla libertà*, Rome, Città Nuova, 2012.
111. PIEVANI, T. (2006), *Creazione senza Dio*, Turin, Einaudi.
112. PIEVANI, T. (2007), *In difesa di Darwin*, Milan, Bompiani.
113. PIEVANI, T. (2010), *La teoria dell'evoluzione*, Bologna, il Mulino.
114. PIEVANI, T. (2011), *La vita inaspettata*, Milan, Raffaello Cortina Editore.
115. PIEVANI, T. (2014), *Evoluti e abbandonati*, Turin, Einaudi.
116. POLKINGHORNE, J. (1989), *Scienza e provvidenza*, Tr. it. Milan, Sperling& Kupfer, 1993.
117. POLKINGHORNE, J., *Science and Providence: God's Interaction with the World*, Conshohoken PA, Templeton Press, 2005.
118. POLKINGHORNE, J. (1998), *Credere in Dio nell'età della scienza*, Tr. it. Milan, Raffaello Cortina Editore, 2000.
119. POLKINGHORNE, J., *Belief in God in an Age of Science*, New Haven, Yale University Press, 2003.
120. POTOK, C. (1978), *Storia degli Ebrei*, Tr. it. Garzanti, Milano 2003.
121. POTOK, C., *Chaim Potok's History of the Jews*, New York, Knopf, 1978.
122. RAVASI, G. (2003), *Breve storia dell'anima*, Milan, Mondadori.
123. RAVASI, G.F. (2013), *Darwin e il Papa. Il falso dilemma tra evoluzione e creazione*, Bologna, EDB.
124. ROVELLI, C. (2014), *Sette brevi lezioni di fisica*, Milan, Adelphi.
125. ROVELLI, C., *Seven Brief Lessons on Physics*, New York, Riverhead/Penguin, 2016.
126. ROVELLI, C. (2014), *La realtà non è come ci appare*, Milan, Raffaello Cortina Editore.
127. ROVELLI, C. (2018), *Reality Is Not What It Seems. The Journey to Quantum Gravity*, New York, Riverhead/Penguin, 2018.
128. ROVELLI, C. (2017), *L'ordine del tempo*, Milan, Adelphi.
129. ROVELLI, C., *The Order of Time*, New York, Riverhead/Penguin, 2019.
130. SATLOW, M.L. (2014), *E il Signore parlò a Mosé. Come la Bibbia divenne sacra*, Tr. it., Turin, Bollati e Boringhieri, 2015.

131. SATLOW, M.L., *How the Bible Became Holy*, New Haven, Yale University Press, 2014.
132. SCHNIEDEWIND, W.M. (2004), *Come la Bibbia divenne un libro*, Tr. it., Brescia, Queriniana, 2008.
133. SCHNIEDEWIND, W.M., *How the Bible Became a Book: The Textualization of Ancient Israel*, Cambridge, Cambridge University Press, 2015.
134. SCHRODINGER, E. (1944), *Cos'è la vita?* Tr. it., Milan, Adelphi, 1995.
135. SCHRODINGER, E., *What is Life? With Mind and Matter and Autobiographical Sketches*, Cambridge, Cambridge University Press, 2012.
136. SEARLE, J.R. (1992), *La riscoperta della mente*, Tr. it. Bollati Boringhieri, Torino 1994.
137. SEARLE, J.R., *The Rediscovery of the Mind*, Boston, MIT Press, 1992.
138. SINDONI, E. (2011), *Siamo soli nell'Universo?* Editrice San Raffaele, Milano.
139. SKA, J.L. (1998), *Introduzione alla lettura del Pentateuco*, EDB, Bologna 2000.
140. SKA, J.L. (2000), *La Parola di Dio nei racconti degli uomini*, Assisi, Cittadella Editrice.
141. SKA, J.L. (2006), *I volti insoliti di Dio*, EDB, Bologna.
142. STEFANI, P. (2004), *La Bibbia*, il Mulino, Bologna.
143. SWIMME, B. TUCKER, M. E. (2011), *Il viaggio dell'universo*, Tr. it., Rome, Fazi Editore, 2013.
144. SWIMME, B. TUCKER, M. E., *Journey of the Universe*, New Haven, Yale University Press, 2011.
145. SWINBURNE, R. (2010), *Esiste un Dio?* Tr. it., Vatican City, Pontificia Università Lateranense, 2013.
146. TANZELLA-NITTI, G. (2002) *"Antropico, Principio"*, in *Dizionario Interdisciplinare di Scienza e Fede*, ed. G. Tanzella-Nitti and A. Strumia, on line at http://disf.org/dizionario.
147. TANZELLA-NITTI, G. (2010) *Cosmologia fisica e domanda sul fondamento dell'essere*, Rome, Seminario 23 ottobre 2010, Incontri su Scienza e fede del Centro Documentazione Interdisciplinare di Scienza e fede, online at www.youtube.com/watch?v=xjJLvb85RnI.
148. TANZELLA-NITTI, G. (2010) *Una lettura dell'evoluzione cosmico-biologica: Il Principio Antropico e le sue implicazioni teologiche*, online pdf. all'indirizzo: http://www.tanzella-nitti.it/sites/default/files/media/pdf/Anthropic_Principle.pdf.
149. TANZELLA-NITTI, G. (2012) *Theologia Physica? Razionalità scientifica e domanda su Dio*, in "Hermeneutica", *Nuovi ateismi e antiche idolatrie*, Brescia, Morcelliana.
150. TANZELLA-NITTI, *Faith, Reason, and the Natural Sciences: The Challenge of the Natural Sciences in the Work of Theologians*, Aurora CO, The Davies Group Publishers, 2009.
151. TATTERSALL, I. (1998), *Il cammino dell'uomo*, Tr. it., Turin, Bollati Boringhieri, 2011.
152. TATTERSALL, I., *The Human Odyssey: Four Million Years of Human Evolution*, New York, Macmillan, 1993.

153. TATTERSALL, I. (2008), *Il mondo prima della storia*, Tr. it., Milan, Raffaello Cortina Editore, 2009.
154. TOMASELLO, M. (2016), *Storia naturale della morale umana*, Milan, Raffaello Cortina Editore.
155. TOMASELLO, M., *A Natural History of Human Morality*, Cambridge MA, Harvard University Press, 2018.
156. TONELLI, G. (2016), *La nascita imperfetta delle cose*, Milan, Rizzoli.
157. TONELLI, G. *La scoperta del bosone di Higgs e il suo impatto sulla nostra visione dell'Universo*, Conferenza tenuta alla Festa Scienza e Filosofia di Foligno, il 3 maggio 2016, online at https://www.youtube.com/watch?v=c1SQq2XY1r4
158. TONELLI, G. (2017), *Cercare mondi*, Milan, Rizzoli.
159. VOTANO, L. (2015), *Il fantasma dell'universo. Che cos'è il neutrino*, Rome, Carocci Editore.
160. WALZER, M. (1985), *Esodo e rivoluzione*, Tr. it., Milan, Feltrinelli, 1986.
161. WALZER, M., *Exodus and Revolution*, New York, Basic Books, 1986.
162. WEINBERG, S. (2015), *Spiegare il mondo*, Tr. it. Milan, Mondadori.
163. WEINBERG, S., *To Explain the World: The Discovery of Modern Science*, New York, Harper Perennial, 2016.
164. WILCZEK, F. (2015), *Una bellissima domanda*, Tr. it., Turin, Einaudi, 2016.
165. WILCZEK, F., *A Beautiful Question: Finding Nature's Deep Design*, Allen Lane/ Penguin, 2015.
166. ZENGER, E. (1983), *Il Dio dell'Esodo*, Tr. it. Bologna, EDB.

Notes

Notes to the Introduction

[1] Fyodor Dostoevsky, *The Brothers Karamazov*, trans. Pevear & Volokhonsky, New York, Farar, Straus & Giroux, 2002.

[2] King James Bible, Job 9:24; 10: 20-22.

[3] Regarding psychology and freedom, Cfr. Michela Dall'Aglio Maramotti, *I legami della libertà*, Bologna, Il Mulino, 2007

[4] The complex question of free will remains wide open: some scholars maintain that it is a sophisticated product of our mind, while others see it as a product of culture without any foundation in objective reality. Cognitive scientist Daniel Dennett, for example, holds that free will is real, but not in the same sense as the law of gravity. Gravity is independent of our existence, while free will is "an evolved creation of human activities and beliefs". Real, that is the way music or money are. This book will not concern itself with defining free will.

[5] Roberta De Monticelli, *La novità di ognuno*, Milan, Garzanti, 2012 (2009), 81-82. De Monticelli explains, "The problem of free will is a particular case of the more general problem of whether the things that appear, which come from our experience of the world and ourselves, are also real; that is whether the immense depository of our explicit or implicit beliefs and our tacit or recognized knowledge of the datum of the world of life have some foundation in truth. . . whether phenomena have some foundation in re. Or whether the opposite is the case, and we . . . are nothing more than the product of dreams projected by our brains. . ." (82).

[6] Etty Hillesum, *Diario 1941-1943*, Milan, Adelphi, 133.

Notes to Chapter One

[7] Hans Jonas, *Sull'orlo dell'abisso. Conversazioni sul rapporto tra uomo e natura*, Turin, Einaudi, 58.

[8] A layperson who defined himself as, "secular but not a secularist, a christian free of bonds," Pareyson was a scholar of Kierkegaard, Schelling, Pascal, Jaspers, and Heidegger. He was a passionate reader of literature and poetry, especially Melville, Leopardi, Manzoni, Donne, and above all Dostoyevsky, on whose work he published extensively. His students included Umberto Eco, Gianni Vattimo, Guido Ceronetti, and Sergio Givone. The existential drama of humanity, the ambiguity of the real, and the role of freedom were central themes in his work.

[9] Pareyson argues for this fascinating thesis of major intellectual impact in his final work, *Ontologia della libertà* (Turin, Einaudi, 2000), which remained incomplete at his death and was released posthumously in a version edited by his students.

[10] L. Pareyson, *Essere, Libertà, Ambiguità*, Milan, Mursia, 1998, 52.

[11] K. Jaspers, *La fede filosofica*, Milan, Raffaello Cortina 2005, 89 (*Philosophical Faith and Revelation*, New York, Harper & Row, 1967).

[12] L. Pareyson, *Ontologia della libertà*, 137.

[13] L. Pareyson, *Essere, Libertà, Ambiguità*, 185.

[14] L. Pareyson, *Ontologia della libertà*, 141.

[15] K. Jaspers, *La fede filosofica*, 91. On the fact that philosophical discourse on God can only be indirect, cfr. L. Pareyson, *Ontologia della libertà*, 139.

[16] L. Pareyson, *Essere Libertà Ambiguità*, 72.

[17] This proposal is close to one made by Nicolai Berdjaev (1874-1948), an author whose sensibility resembles that of Pareyson: "The problem of freedom . . . concerns the fundamental principles of being and life. The very perception of being depends on and is preceded by freedom. Freedom is a spiritual and religious category." *Filosofia dello spirito libero*, Milan, San Paolo, 203 (*Freedom and the Spirit*, London, G. Bles: Century Press, 1935).

[18] Pareyson: "By virtue of its physical reality and the transcendence that typifies it, the symbol is thus inexhaustibly abyssal, preserving the radical unspeakability of transcendence. Only through myth can one reach to the heart of reality, and only through a symbol can it be at least provisionally figured or represented." *Ontologia della libertà*, 112. On this theme, see the first chapter of the second part of Pareyson's book.

[19] L. Pareyson, *Ontologia della libertà*, 131-134.

[20] *Ibidem*, 283.

[21] Physicist Carlo Tonelli has made this observation in numerous conferences.

[22] Arbitrary means absolute: it is the will that wants, not by chance or capriciously, but solely because it so wills.

[23] "The world is real; this reality means gratuitous . . . something that is and could potentially not be. But. . . this tells us little, because it would be purely and simply the concept of contingency. There is something more: Reality is something supererogatory, purely gratuitous, wholly unmotivated. It is truly a gift and only a gift. Reality as such emerges from freedom, it is bound in freedom, bound in will; that which makes it be is an act of volition. It's not enough simply to say "something that is and could potentially not be", because this still doesn't explain how it is that it is. We can only explain how it is that it is by taking account of its gratuitousness, recognizing it as the fruit of freedom. Freedom is the true and proper origin, the true and proper abyss, the true and proper inexhaustibility." L. Pareyson, *Essere Libertà Ambiguità*, Milan, Mursia 1998, 88-89.

[24] L. Pareyson, *Ontologia della libertà*, 22.

Notes to Chapter Two

[25] *Ibidem*, 283.

[26] Edoardo Boncinelli (with Luigi Offeddu), *Prodigi quotidiani*, Milan, Boroli Editore 2005, 47.

[27] David Jou, *Riscrivere la Genesi*, Rome, Castelvecchi, 2009, 38-39.

[28] Carlo Rovelli, *La realtà non è come ci appare*, Milan, Raffaello Cortina Editore, 2014, 71-72 (*Reality is Not What It Seems. The Journey to Quantum Gravity*, New York, Riverhead Books, 2018).

[29] *Ibidem*, 66, 68. See the appendix to Chapter 2.

[30] *Ibidem*, 81.

[31] While studying electromagnetic power, Michael Faraday (1791-1867) intuited the existence of an entity, called a field, in which bodies move. "Faraday's intuition was this: we must not think . . . of forces acting directly among objects distant one from another. Instead, we should think of a real entity diffused everywhere in space that comes to be modified by electric and magnetic bodies and which in turn makes the electric and magnetic bodies act (pushing and pulling them). This entity intuited by Faraday is today called a 'field'. What then is the 'field'? Faraday imagines it as formed by bands of extremely (infinitely) subtle lines that fill space. A giant invisible spiderweb that fills everything around us. He calls these lines "lines of force" because in some way they are lines that 'carry power': they carry electric force and magnetic force from place to place, as though they were cables that pull and push. . . . Thus, two charges that are at a certain distance one from another neither attract or repel one another directly, but do so through a medium that stands between them." *Ibidem*, 50-51. Einstein's metaphor of the mollusk, *Ibidem*, 73.

[32] Lucia Votano, *Il fantasma dell'universo. Che cos'è il neutrino*, Rome, Carocci 2015, 18-19.

[33] Edoardo Boncinelli, *Prodigi quotidiani*, cit., 44-45.

[34] Stephen W. Hawking, *La grande storia del tempo*, Milan, BUR 2015, 85-86.

[35] See the appendix to Chapter Two.

[36] See the appendix to Chapter Two.

[37] Carlo Rovelli, *La realtà non è come ci appare*, cit., 49. (*Reality is Not What It Seems.*, cit.).

[38] The other particles are the gluon, which mediates the strong interaction that binds the nucleus of the atom; bosons w and z are mediators of the weak force, thus responsible for radioactive decay..

[39] Particle of spin 0, which does not decay.

[40] A phase diagram is a diagram that demonstrates a phase transition, that is, the transformation in a physical system from one state (phase) to another, such as the phase change water/ice/vapor. As for the Universe, the change from a state in which quarks were free to one in which they are bound in protons and neutrons was a phase transition.

[41] Guido Tonelli, "La scoperta del bosone di Higgs e il suo impatto sulla nostra visione dell'Universo", a paper presented at the Festa Scienza e Filosofia di Foligno, May 3, 2016; available on youtube at https://www.youtube.com/watch?v=c1SQq2XY1r4

[42] Bill Bryson, *Breve storia di quasi tutto*, Milan, TEA, 24. (*A Short History of Nearly Everything*, New York, Broadway Books, 2003).

[43] David Jou, *Riscrivere la Genesi*, cit., 244.

[44] "The world of the small is thus populated by fleeting, mysterious entities that obey iron but incomprehensible laws." E. Boncinelli, *Alla ricerca delle leggi di Dio*, Milan, Rizzoli, 2014, 215.

[45] The anecdote is recounted by Carlo Rovelli in *Reality is Not What It Seems*, cit., 117-118.

[46] "In quantum mechanics, no object has a definite position except when it bumps into something else. To describe it halfway between one interaction and another, an abstract mathematical function is used that lives not in real space, but in abstract mathematical spaces. Still worse, these leaps with which every object passes from one interaction to another don't take place predictably, but largely by chance. It is impossible to predict where an electron will appear anew; we can only calculate the probability that it will appear here or there. Probability thus crops up in the heart of

physics, where everything had seemed regulated by precise, unequivocal, inescapable laws." Carlo Rovelli, *Sette brevi lezioni di fisica*, Milan, Adelphi, 2014, 26-27 (*Seven Brief Lessons in Physics*, New York, Riverhead/Penguin, 2016).

[47] "In the act of measurement, 'the packet of waves collapses,' that is, one of the many possible results takes place in an entirely unpredictable way, essentially without any cause. The inability to know in advance the results of a quantum measurement implies the admission that openness toward the future is built into the structure of the world, at the root of its constitutive elements. In the intervals between the diverse operations of measurement, a quantum mechanical system is represented by a wave function that evolves without hiccups, which is an expression of potentiality. . . rather than a specification of actuality." John Polkinghorne, *Scienza e provvidenza*, Milan, Sperling & Kupfer, 1993, 124 (*Science and Providence: God's Interaction with the World*, Conshohoken, PA, Templeton Press, 2005).

[48] "The atom thus turns out to be quite a bit different from the image many people had of it. The atom doesn't orbit around the nucleus like a planet around the sun; instead it appears more amorphous than a cloud. The 'shell' of the atom is not a hard, shiny casing the way illustrations sometimes encourage us to believe, but simply the most peripheral of these clouds of electrons with uncertain outlines. . ." Bill Bryson, *Breve storia di quasi tutto*, cit., 164 (Bill Bryson, *A Short History of Nearly Everything*, New York, Broadway Books, 2003).

[49] ". . . it takes so much imagination to try to figure out what the world is really like," Michelle Feynman, ed., *The Quotable Feynman*, Princeton, Princeton University Press, 2015, 83 (*Le battute memorabilia di Feynman*, Italian trans., Milan, Adelphi, 2017).

[50] "Color as we perceive it is our psychophysical reaction of the nerve signal generated by the receptors of our eyes, which distinguish electromagnetic waves of different frequencies." Carlo Rovelli, *Reality is Not What It Seems*, 60. Color is born from light. The light that strikes an object is partially absorbed depending on what it consists of. The non-absorbed part is reflected and transmitted to chromatic receptors within the human eye. These receptors transform the absorbed light into impulses that run through nerve pathways to reach the brain, where they are interpreted: thus is born a chromatic impression. From the purely biological viewpoint, color is thus generated in the eye of the observer and constitutes a sensorial impression.

[51] "the idea occurs that . . . our way of seeing them has little relation to what they really are," E. Boncinelli, *Alla ricerca delle leggi di Dio*, cit., 183.

[52] Carlo Rovelli, *La realtà non è come ci appare*, cit. 105 (*Reality is Not What It Seems.* cit.).

[53] *Ibidem*, 116.

[54] David Jou, *Riscrivere la Genesi*, cit., 158.

Notes to Chapter Three

[55] Giulio Giorello, Elio Sindoni, *Un mondo di mondi*, Milan, Raffaello Cortina Editore, 2016, 85.

[56] *Ibidem*, 88-89. "Nature has favored life on our planet also for another peculiarity: the Earth possesses a magnetic field, absent on the moon and on Venus and very weak on Mars. . . The most credited hypothesis is that the terrestrial magnetic field is due to the structure of our globe, that is, the circulation and convection of molten iron, faster in the external part and slower in the interior. The terrestrial magnetic field is essential for life: it extends for dozens of kilometers into the space

around the Earth, forming the so-called magnetosphere, and it acts on loaded particles coming from the Sun, especially on protons and electrons, deviating their course and thus impeding a bombardment of the surface which would seriously damage living organisms." *Ibidem*, 89-90.

[57] Hans Jonas (1903-1993), was the author of important books in Twentieth century philosophy, such as *The Imperative of Responsibility* (1979) or *The Concept of God After Auschwitz* (1984), a brief but fundamental meditation of the possibility of believing in the goodness of God after the tragedy of the Shoah, and *Organismo e libertà. Verso una biologia filosofica* (*Organismus und Freiheit. Ansätze zu einer philosophischen Biologie*. Göttingen: Vandenhoeck & Ruprecht, 1973). In English: http://hans-jonas-edition.de/wp-content/uploads/2016/10/KGA_Hans-Jonas-Kontext-Bd.-I1-Organism-and-Freedom.pdf.

[58] Christian De Duve defines metabolism as "a chemical whirlpool. . . in which thousands of reactions allow the substances present to undergo modifications of varied nature." Christian De Duve, *Come evolve la vita*, Milan, Raffaello Cortina Editore, 2003, 11.

[59] Hans Jonas, *Organismo e libertà. Verso una biologia filosofica*, Turin, Einaudi, 1999, Author's Preface, 3 (*The Phenomenon of Life. Towards a Philosophical Biology*, New York, Harper & Row, 1966).

[60] *Ibidem*, 9. Jonas's interest in the distinction between organic and inorganic life was born from his study of the ethical problems arising from the relation between modernity and technology. It is impossible, in fact, to speak of ethics and responsibility in relation to life without having first defined in some way life itself, in its most primeval form; that is, how it is different from inorganic matter.

[61] It is a widely held opinion that the ability to "take from the environment the necessary materials and energy, and return waste products to it," is a necessary requirement for life, from the most primitive proto-cells. Cfr. Christian De Duve, *Come evolve la vita*, cit., 92. (*Life Evolving: Molecules, Mind, and Meaning*, London, Oxford University Press, 2002).

[62] Cfr. Brian Swimme, Mary E. Tucker, *The Journey of the Universe*. New Haven, Yale University Press, 2011. See the appendix to Chapter Three (*Il viaggio dell'universo*, Italian trans. Rome, Fazi Editore, 2013).

[63] "Only life has purpose, beyond mere cause, because it is the only reality that has an interest in its own maintenance and the tools needed to sustain it. . . life cannot be understood except by approaching the concepts of purpose, value, and good in a biological, organic sense." Leonardo Paris, *Sulla libertà*, Rome, Città Nuova, 158.

[64] Cfr. Hans Jonas, *Organismo e libertà*, cit., 117 (*The Phenomenon of Life*. cit.).

[65] *Ibidem*, 119

[66] *Ibidem*, 117. On the basis of this conviction, Jonas moves on to a consideration of the question of human and divine freedom together.

[67] Peter M. Hoffmann, *Gli ingranaggi di Dio*, Milan, Bollati Boringhieri, 294-295.

[68] See the appendix to Chapter Three.

[69] Stephen J. Gould, *Wonderful Life. The Burgess Shale and the Nature of History*, New York, W.W. Norton, 1989, 14 (*La vita meravigliosa*, Milan, Feltrinelli, 1995).

[70] Monod presented his viewpoint in an influential book, *Il caso e la necessità* (1971).

[71] Fritjof Capra, Pier Luigi Luisi, *Vita e natura. Una visione sistemica*, Sansepolcro, Aboca, 2014, 270.

[72] The term for the lancet-fish, amphioxus, generically indicates the Cephalochordata, filtering marine organisms of modest dimensions and devoid of limbs. The amphioxus is the first step in the

scale of vertebrates. The story of the discovery of Pikaia is told in many books. I have made particular reference to S.J. Gould, *La vita meravigliosa*, cit. (*Wonderful Life*, cit.), and to Telmo Pievani,
La vita inaspettata, Milan, Raffaello Cortina editore, 2011.

[73] This is the most ancient class of the phylum of the annelids, vermiform animals with a seg-
mented cylindrical body, prevalently but no exclusively marine (the common earthworm, for example, is an annelid). The phylum (pl. phyla) is a subdivision below the kingdom (animal and
vegetable). Each subdivision consists of groups considered similar on the basis of morphological
organization. The principles categories, as regards human beings, are: domain eukaryotes (eukary-
otic cells with a nucelus and cytoplasm); kingdom, animal; phylum, chordates (with a dorsal column); subphylum, vertebrates (with a bony or cartilaginous backbone); subclass, tetrapods (with
four limbs); class, mammals; order, primates; family, hominids; genus, homo; species, sapiens.

[74] Stephen J. Gould, *La vita meravigliosa*, cit., p.238 (*Wonderful Life*, cit.).

[75] With the exception of trilobites, among fossils there are only few examples. "Everything we
have learned from the most beautiful and detailed monographs on the paleontology of the Twentieth
century tells us that the Burgess victims were adequately specialized and highly skilled." S. J. Gould,
La vita meravigliosa, 244 (*Wonderful Life*, cit.).

[76] *Ibidem*, 294.

[77] Telmo Pievani, *La vita inaspettata*, cit., 95.

[78] ". . . other chordates, as yet undiscovered, must have inhabited Cambrian seas. But I suspect,
from the rarity of *Pikaia* in the Burgess and the absence of chordates in the other Lower Paleozoic
Lagerstätten (fossil deposits), however, that our phylum did not rank among the great Cambrian
success stories, and chordates faced a tenuous future in Burgess times. *Pikaia* is the missing and final
link in our story of contingency—the direct connection between Burgess decimation and eventual
human evolution. . . If *Pikaia* does not survive in the replay, we are wiped out of future history—all
of us, from shark to robin to orangutan." Stephen J. Gould, *Wonderful Life*, p.322-323 (*La vita
meravigliosa*, cit.).

[79] Stephen J. Gould, *La vita meravigliosa*, cit., 238 (*Wonderful Life*, cit.). Explaining the importance of Burgess, Gould wrote, "I believe that the reconstructed Burgess fauna, interpreted by the
theme of replaying life's tape, offers powerful support for this different view of life: any replay of the
tape would lead evolution down a pathway radically different from the road actually taken. But the
consequent differences in outcome do not imply that evolution is senseless and without meaningful
pattern; the divergent route of the replay would be just as interpretable, just as explainable *after* the
fact, as the actual road. But the diversity of possible itineraries does demonstrate that the eventual results cannot be predicted at the outset. Each step proceeds for cause, but no finale can be specified at
the start, and none would ever occur a second time in the same way, because any pathway proceeds
through thousands of improbable stages." *Ibidem*, 51.

[80] *Ibidem*, 48.

[81] Telmo Pievani, *La vita inaspettata*, cit., 115 (*Wonderful Life*, cit.).

[82] Cfr. Francisco J. Ayala, *Il dono di Darwin alla scienza e alla religione*, Milan, Edizioni San
Paolo, 2009. Stephen J. Gould, *La vita meravigliosa*, cit., 298 (*Wonderful Life*, cit.).

[83] Telmo Pievani, *La vita inaspettata*, cit., 115 (*Wonderful Life*, cit.).

[84] *Ibidem*, 110.

[85] Stephen J. Gould, *Wonderful Life*, cit., 323 (*La vita meravigliosa*, cit.).

[86] An interesting hypothesis on the role of collaboration in human evolution is expressed by the

American evolutionary psychologist Michael Tomasello in *Storia naturale della morale umana*, Milan, Raffaello Cortina, 2016.

[87] Telmo Pievani, *La vita inaspettata*, cit., 63.

[88] These were large multicellular organisms "shaped like pancakes, with soft bodies", as described by Stephen J. Gould, whose importance resides in the fact that they are the only proof we have of multicellular life before the second great explosion of life circa 30 million years later, at the beginning of the Cambrian Era, with organisms very different from the preceding Ediacara, from which they do not seem to be descended. Telmo Pievani, *La vita inaspettata*, cit., 65.

[89] The most extraordinary thing to Gould is that virtually all phyla—all types of anatomical organization—which still exist on Earth came about at that time, plus an extraordinary number of forms now extinct. All the fundamental body plans would have appeared, according to Gould, during the Cambrian explosion. Subsequent findings and studies have confirmed and added detail and nuance to Gould's hypotheses, which has been widely accepted.

[90] Telmo Pievani, *La vita inaspettata*, cit., 65.

[91] "That 'unexplainable' exuberance of multicellular organisms with hard shells and the absence of sure evidence of a preparatory phase raised doubts about his idea that evolution was necessarily slow and uniform. With the intellectual honesty to anticipate the objections of his adversaries, in the sixth edition of The Origin of Species, in 1872, he admits that circumstances in the Cambrian might 'constitute a valid argument against the opinions here expressed'." Telmo Pievani, *La vita inaspettata*, cit., 65-66.

[92] Ian Tattersall, *Il mondo prima della storia*, cit., 10.

[93] Giorgio Manzi, *Il grande racconto dell'evoluzione umana*, Bologna, il Mulino, 2013, 77.

[94] Telmo Pievani, *La vita inaspettata*, cit., 136 (he cites Giorgio Manzi, *L'evoluzione umana*, Bologna, il Mulino, 2007, 8).

[95] *Ibidem.*

[96] This example comes from Fritjof Capra, Pier Luigi Luisi, *Vita e natura*, cit., 305-306, sgg.

[97] We share 98 percent of our DNA with the African anthropomorphs, which is hardly surprising, considering that we stood on the same evolutionary branch for 99.9999997 percent of history. It may be more surprising to learn that we share 40 percent of our DNA with the banana! "All mammals share a common ancestor with reptiles, which lived 300 million years ago, all vertebrates share a common ancestor that lived 500 million years ago, and so on," Telmo Pievani, *La teoria dell'evoluzione*, cit., 14. The many names subsequently given to hominid remains and the variability of dates to which scholars ascribe common ancestors of diverse genus (in particular the hominid-anthropomorph ancestor, from seven to four million years ago) give witness to the extremely rapid progress in paleontology and related fields in recent decades.

[98] The DNA of modern humans derive from a single (variant) female aplotype that emerged in Africa some time between 290,000 and 140,000 years ago. . . Various groups of researchers, furthermore, are converging on the idea of an African ancestor of Homo sapiens that originated little more than 150-200,000 years ago." Ian Tattersall, *Il mondo prima della storia*, cit, 119.

[99] The term "race" is entirely inappropriate when speaking of humans because it was coined exclusively in reference to the breeding of animals and the artificial creation of animal races by humans.

[100] Ian Tattersall, *Il cammino dell'uomo*, Turin, Bollati Boringhieri, 2011, 169 (*The Human Odyssey: Four Million Years of Human Evolution*, New York, Macmillan, 1993).

[101] It may be that this conviction will one day turn out to be a prejudice due to our innate superiority complex. At the current state of knowledge, in any case, it appears to be the case.

[102] This is how experts interpret the signs of the artists' hands which are common on the walls of the era's caves; a way of recognizing oneself and being recognized by others.

[103] See the Appendix to Chapter Three.

[104] Ian Tattersall, *Il mondo prima della storia*, cit, 134-135.

[105] Leonardo Paris, *Sulla libertà*, cit., 94-95. Evolutionary psychologist Michael Lewis describes self-consciousness as "the ability to think about who we are today in terms of the past and the future." Joseph LeDoux, *Ansia*, Milan, Raffaello Cortina Editore, 2016, 279.

[106] See the Appendix to Chapter Three. On the formation and details of human consciousness see also Joseph LeDoux, *Ansia*; M.Tomasello, *Storia naturale della morale umana*; Frans de Waal, *Siamo così intelligenti da capire l'intelligenza degli animali?*, Milan, Raffaello Cortina Editore, 2016.

[107] The last common ancestor of sapiens and neanderthal seems to have lived circa 700-500.000 years ago.

[108] Ian Tattersall, *Il mondo prima della storia*, cit., 114.

[109] On symbolic thought among Neanderthals: "The most remarkable example comes from the Sungir' site in Russian [northeast of Moscow] dated 28 ka, where two quite young males and one male of approximately 60 years of age (no other human species had heretofore reached such an age) were buried with an astounding richness of accoutrements. Each of the deceased was dressed in clothing sewn with more than 3,000 mammoth tusk pearls (experiments determined that each pearl would have been worked for over an hour) and with incised pendants, bracelets, and shell necklaces. The two youths, buried head to head, were flanked by two meter-long mammoth tusks, which, amazing, had been straightened by a procedure still not understood. . . . One thing is certain: the awareness of the intevitability of death is closely connected to spirituality, and Cro-Magnon burials demonstrate evidence of both. Here we have the first incontrovertible evidence of religious experience." Ian Tattersall, *Il cammino dell'uomo*, cit., 15-16 (*The Human Odyssey,* cit.).

[110] Telmo Pievani, *La vita inaspettata*, cit., p.38.

Notes to Chapter Four

[111] Luigi Pareyson dedicates some of his most intense and visionary pages to this theme.

[112] As observed concerning the arbitrary characteristics of divine will, we speak here of a will that does not express itself by chance, but by simple will itself.

[113] Although there are shadings of meaning between being and existing, they will be used here for the most part as synonyms.

[114] In some biblical passages, death is expressly not attributed to God, while in other passages God claims to bestow both life and death..

[115] Cfr. Amir D. Aczel, *Perché la scienza non nega Dio*, Milan, Raffaello Cortina Editore, 2015, 66.

[116] According to the kabbalistic doctrine of *tzimtzum* (meaning contraction or retraction), God must have sacrificed something of himself in order to provide space for the world. This doctrine was recalled by Hans Jonas in *The Concept of God After Auschwitz* to account for God's voluntary and effectual renunciation of his own omnipotence.

[117] Luigi Pareyson, *Ontologia della libertà*, cit., 136.

[118] "The clash of opposites is not a logical struggle with a logical outcome, as in Hegel; rather it is a history, and thus free, because what characterizes history is freedom, while a logical process is characterized by necessity." Luigi Pareyson, *Essere Libertà Ambiguità*, cit., 32.

[119] Luigi Pareyson, *Ontologia della libertà*, cit., 273.

[120] See in particular Salvatore Natoli, *L'esperienza del dolore*, Milan, Feltrinelli, 1986.

[121] See the appendix to Chapter Four.

[122] Luigi Pareyson, *Ontologia della libertà*, cit., 226.

[123] "Strictly speaking, God is the author neither of good nor evil, because God does not so much do good; rather, God is goodness. As for evil, rather than doing evil God contains it, and contains it as possibility, which is thus not precisely evil because it is not reality but merely possibility, which furthermore is defeated and dormant." Luigi Pareyson, *Ibidem*, 96.

[124] *Ibidem*, p.265.

[125] Luigi Pareyson, *Essere Libertà Ambiguità*, cit., 159.

[126] *Ibidem*, 178-179.

[127] Luigi Pareyson, *Ontologia della libertà*, cit., p.183.

[128] *Ibidem*, 185.

[129] "Not being + liberty = nothingness: this is the arithmetic of freedom. By virtue of the vigor of freedom, vacuous and dead nothingness becomes operative, as evil." *Ibidem*, 258.

[130] *Ibidem*, 233-234.

[131] *Ibidem*, 11.

[132] *Ibidem*, 22.

[133] *Ibidem*, 259-260.

[134] *Ibidem*, 269.

[135] Psychologist Viktor Frankl has written brilliantly on this subject.

[136] Luigi Pareyson, *Ontologia della libertà*, cit., 13. Due to this, freedom and situation must not be seen as opposed; rather, "in the concreteness of human action, [in which] they are unified and manifest alternatingly: the situation is already qualified by the initiative of freedom, and freedom (concrete, incarnate, situated) takes on form in the situation. . . . [in respect of which] freedom is at least free, not to exit from the situation, but to adopt it or rebel against it. Rebellion leads nowhere except into the tangle of non-acceptance, of internal repudiation; the situation, which could have become possibility, a vehicle, instead becomes an obstacle, a prison." *Ibidem*.

[137] Jean d'Ormesson, *Che cosa strana è il mondo*, Florence, Barbès Editore, 2011, 240.

Notes to Chapter Five

[138] Edoardo Boncinelli puts the problem this way: "Material reality may have an autonomous life, but the consciousness of it may not. It is the fruit of a continuous process punctuated by new discoveries, including conceptual ones, which all together constitute over time what we call truth. There is no established truth, but it is convenient for us to believe that it exists somewhere and that someone may know it in its entirety, even perhaps today. . . Those who want to believe that the truth, or rather Truth, is out there somewhere, like to consider themselves liberated. If a truth existed today—and a future—that would mean there is no space for freedom, neither for us nor for things."

Edoardo Boncinelli, *Alla ricerca delle leggi*, cit., 18. Still, one could object that the very truth that he claims would impede freedom is freedom itself. If by the term freedom he means a sort of deterministic necessity, then he would be right.

[139] John Polkinghorne, *Scienza e provvidenza*, cit., 59 (*Science and Providence*, cit.). On the freedom of the Universe, see also Fritjof Capra, Pier Luigi Luisi, *Vita e natura*, cit.

[140] Polkinghorne, *Scienza*, cit., 50.

[141] Alister McGrath, *La grande domanda*, Milano Bollati Boringheri, 87

[142] Christian De Duve, *Polvere vitale*, Longanesi, Milano 1998, 15; the citation is from Vito Mancuso, *Il principio passione*, Garzanti, Milano 2013, 145.

[143] This is a sequence of phenomena that seems to depend closely, "on numerous other conditions of a structural rather than evolutionary character which involve the properties of elementary particles, atomic energy levels, chemical links, and certain of the major physical constants. A fact of extreme interest is that the numerical values of the four constants of interaction turn out to be already fixed within a range of time of approximately 10^{-6} from the horizon of the Big Bang, that is, the epoch in which electromagnetic forces differentiates itself from the other three constants, and the properties of the protons and neutrons are by then determined." Giuseppe Tanzella-Nitti, "Antropico, Principio", in the *Dizionario Interdisciplinare di Scienza e Fede*, eds G. Tanzella-Nitti and A. Strumia, online at: http://disf.org/dizionario. Cfr. also Alistair McGrath, *La grande domanda*, Bollati Boringheri, Torino 2016, 91.

[144] G. Tanzella-Nitti, "Antropico, Principio", cit.

[145] This was elaborated for the first time in 1974 by Australian physicist and cosmologist Brandon Carter, but debate became ever more bitter beginning in 1980, year of the publication of *The Anthropic Cosmological Principle*, by John Barrow (mathematician and cosmologist) and Frank Tipler (physicist and mathematician).

[146] See the Appendix to Chapter Five. Cfr. Tanzella-Nitti, *Dizionario*, cit.

[147] "This last implication cannot be established on a scientific level (scientific weakness of the strong formulation) simply because we do not know the conditions and processes such that, given the existence of a physics and chemistry adequate for life (necessary conditions), it is always necessary to conclude that life effectually makes its appearance (sufficient conditions). In other words, the discovery or, also, the physical-mathematic justification of those delicate conditions does not constitute a justification of why life exists and what it is." Tanzella-Nitti, *Dizionario*, cit.

[148] Cfr. Giuseppe Tanzella-Nitti, *Cosmologia fisica e domanda sul fondamento dell'essere*, Seminar, Rom3, October 23, 2010, "Incontri su Scienza e fede del Centro Documentazione Interdisciplinare di Scienza e fede", online at www.youtube.com/watch?v=xjJLvb85RnI.

[149] Cfr. *Ibidem*.

[150] See also Richard Swinburne, *Esiste un Dio?*, Vatican City, Pontificia Universita Lateranense, 2013.

[151] Christian De Duve, *Come evolve la vita*, cit., 400 (*Life Evolving*, cit.).

[152] Cfr. Tanzella-Nitti, "Una lettura dell'evoluzione cosmico-biologica: Il Principio Antropico e le sue implicazioni teologiche", available online at: http://www.tanzella-nitti.it/sites/default/files/media/pdf/Anthropic_Principle.pdf. See the Appendix to Chapter Five. Cfr. Tanzella-Nitti, *Il Principio Antropico e le sue implicazioni teologiche*, cit.

[153] Paul Davies, *Discorso per il premio Templeton*, May, 1995, cited in Antony Flew (with Roy Abraham Varghese) *Dio esiste*, Caltanisetta, Alfa&Omega, 2010, 116. The conclusion of the es-

say which brought him to the attention of a non-specialized audience, Davies claims: "I began by making the claim that science offers a surer path than religion in the search of God. It is my deep conviction that only by understanding the world in all its many aspects—reductionist and holist, mathematical and poetical, through forces, fields, and particles as well as through good and evil— that we will come to understand ourselves and the meaning behind this universe, our home." Paul Davies, *God and the New Physics*, New York, Simon and Schuster, 1983, 229.

[154] Freeman Dyson, *Turbare l'universo*, Milan, Bollati Boringhieri, 1979, 291(*Disturbing the Universe*, New York, Harper & Row, 1979).

[155] Antony Flew, *Dio esiste*, cit., 105.

[156] J. d'Ormesson, *Che cosa strana è il mondo*, cit., 164.

[157] Richard Swinbourne, *Esiste Dio?*, cit., 81.

[158] LeDoux, *Ansia*, cit., 81.

[159] See the Appendix to Chapter Five.

[160] See the Appendix to Chapter Five.

[161] We remember that Jonas was convinced that even in the smallest organic entity there exists and orientation toward life, which, "in the depths of being itself" (*Organismo e libertà*, cit., 116) that a vital principle is in action that tends to transform the inorganic into a living thing. In matter is the potentiality for the generation of life, therefore "the organic prefigures the spiritual already in its most inferior forms and . . . spirit in its maximum extension still remains part of the organic." We might paraphrase his statement, "if 'spirit' is prefigured from the very beginning of the organic, the same must be true of freedom," by inverting the order to read, "if freedom is prefigured from the very beginning of the organic, the same must be true of the spirit." The presence of spirit and freedom remains in the organic, but in our new version freedom comes in fact to be identical with spirit, the most immaterial part of reality. And it belongs to all reality in different measure. The border between matter and immaterial becomes ever more uncertain.

[162] See the Appendix to Chapter Five. Cfr. John R. Searle, *La riscoperta della mente*, Turin, Bollati Boringhieri, 1994 (*The Rediscovery of the Mind*, Boston, MIT Press, 1992).

[163] This is the problem of consciousness: "How can the brain permit us to pass from the electro-chemical to sensation?" John R. Searle, *Il mistero della coscienza*, 21, cited in Leonardo Paris, *Sulla libertà*, cit., 34. Ayala asks the same question: "How do physical-chemical signals transmitted by neurons become psychological events such as thoughts, feelings, and self-awareness? Human beings are the only creature that have self-awareness, that is, the perception of existing as individuals who live for a certain period of time and then die." Francisco Ayala, *Il dono di Darwin*, cit., 140.

[164] Richard Swinburne, *Esiste un Dio?*, cit., 89.

[165] The existence of gravity was finally confirmed by the observation of gravitational waves, which took place after decades of research finally in 2016.

[166] He continues: "If I believe in God, if I force myself to understand the God I love and that I believe created the universe, then the very nature of that universe has something to tell me about that God." Riccardo Chiaberge, *La variabile Dio*, 41 and 119.

[167] Cfr. Carlo Rovelli, *La realtà non è come ci appare*, cit. (*Reality Is Not What It Seems*, cit.).

[168] "To claim that the evolution of consciousness was an inevitable process and to base this assumption on the concept of adaptive convergence is, however, in clear contradiction of the fact that human consciousness has such, in three and a half billion years of the history of life, has evolved one time only! Over an immense stretch of time that corresponds to almost half the duration of the Earth

itself, the experiment of human consciousness remains, in the absence of contrary evidence, unique. And still more unique in that it contradicts the fact that a hair's width kept us on diverse occasions from never evolving at all." Telmo Pievani, *La vita inaspettata*, cit. 134.

[169] Cfr. Leonardo Paris, *Sulla libertà*, 109-110.

[170] Brian Swimme, Mary E.Tucker, *Il viaggio dell'universo*, cit., 12 (*Journey of the Universe*, cit.).

[171] Vito Mancuso, *Il principio passione*, cit., 159.

[172] Vito Mancuso, *Il principio passione*, cit., 133.

[173] "Man is not a genetic machine. In mammals, genes express themselves through interaction with the environment according to complex models that are almost impossible to predict in detail; and the self resides in the details." Francisco Ayala, *Il dono di Darwin*, cit., 157.

[174] Vito Mancuso, *Il principio passione*, cit., 159.

[175] Vito Mancuso, *Il principio passione*, cit., cfr. 385-390.

[176] Michael Gazzaniga maintains that mankind is naturally dualistic: "You think in an intuitive and non-reflexive way that the body and its conscious essence are separate." Michael Gazzaniga, *Human. Quel che ci rende unici*, Milan, Raffaello Cortina Editore, 2009, 336 (*Human. The Science Behind What Makes Your Brain Unique*, New York, Harper Perennial, 2009).

[177] Vito Mancuso, *Il principio passione*, cit., 182.

[178] "Does science consider man merely another type of chimpanzee. . . ? . . . Perhaps that the religious conception of man as a special creature of God is without foundation? The answer is that, by some biological profiles, we are very similar to chimpanzees, but by other equally biological profiles we are quite different, and these differences represent a valid foundation for the religious conception of man as a special creature of God. Francisco Ayala, *Il dono di Darwin*, cit., 153-154 (*Darwin's Gift to Science and Religion*, Washington DC, Joseph Henry Press, 2007).

[179] For Peter M. Hoffman, mankind is "a natural extension of the creativity of the Universe", Peter M. Hoffmann, *Gli ingranaggi di Dio, Dal caos molecolare alla vita*, Turin, Bollati Boringhieri, 2014, 297.

Notes to Chapter 6

[180] Wishing to posit the bases of a theology that permits us to discover the multiplicity of the faces of God, Carmine de Sante, invites us to "read the religious phenomenon by listening to the texts in which it came to be embodied, renouncing the pretense of judging it from an external viewpoint, on the basis of personal or ideological presuppositions that depend on one's own historical era or cultural context." Cfr. Carmine de Sante, *Dio e i suoi volti*, Introduction, Milan, Edizioni San Paolo 2012. And Gianfranco Ravasi states: ". . . apart from religious beliefs, the words, symbols, and ideas of the Bible are also the 'great codex' of all western culture, the fundamental lexicon of our representations and interpretations of reality." G. Ravasi, *Breve storia dell'anima*, Milan, Mondadori, 2003, 71.

[181] "Since all societies possess forms of religion that always accompany of mythology of origins, whose purpose is to explain the relation of humans with the surrounding environment. . . in our conception of God . . . we see more distinctly reflected the human condition." Ian Tattersall, *Il cammino dell'uomo*, cit., p180-181.

[182] In a Catholic Christian context, this opposition I believe to be fundamentally based on the fact that people tend to identify the Church and its precepts with God. This is a misleading identifi-

cation when taken as rigid and absolute, because certainly the Church interprets the divine, but like all human reality, it remains subject to all the limits and cultural conditioning of any society; which God by definition—and I would add fortunately—surpasses.

[183] Abraham J. Heschel, *Il canto della libertà*, Magnano, Edizioni Qiqajon, Comunità di Bose, 1999, 46.

[184] I take this citation from David Jou, *Riscrivere la Genesi*, cit., 219.

[185] Karl Jaspers, *La fede filosofica*, cit., 89 (*Philosophical Faith*, cit.).

[186] Salvatore Natoli, *Il rischio di fidarsi*, Bologna, il Mulino, 2016, 142.

[187] Abraham J. Heschel, *Il canto della libertà*, cit., 46.

[188] This objection was presented to me in a still more totalizing formulation: "What does God have to do with freedom? God is the origin of guilt; we are told to kneel before him, beat our chests and say *mea culpa, mea massima culpa!*" What's transparent here is the memory of a childhood catechism focuses on precepts, transgressions, and a system of reward and punishment. The viewpoint from which we'd like to approach the question is different, my inquiry is metaphysical and philosophical rather than confessional. The objection in any case is legitimate and important, and I hope that what follows may uncover some possible answers.

[189] "Individual life is the presence or manifestation of a will, of a unity of intention, of an interest in and care for the non-self." Abraham J. Heschel, *Il messaggio dei profeti*, Rome, Edizioni Borla, 1993, 79 (*The Prophets*, New York, Harper Perennial, 2001). A person is a subject endowed with a rational nature, capable of autonomy and choice, able to distinguish good from evil, a possessor of rights, worthy of respect, and bearer of dignity for the simple fact of existing (alive, but also dead), intelligent, free, capable of will.

[190] David Jou, *Riscrivere la Genesi*, cit. 248.

[191] In truth the biblical God is much more than this, but entering into this topic would lead us to a spiritual and religious realm which, however interesting and intriguing, does not pertain to our discourse.

[192] Psalm 61 (62).

[193] This is the title of an essay by Bible scholar Jean Louis Ska, *La Parola di Dio nei racconti degli uomini*, Assisi, Cittadella Editrice. Cfr. also Claudio Cianci, *Percorsi della libertà*, Milan-Udine, Mimesis Edizioni, 2012, 87-88.

[194] Abraham J. Heschel, *Crescere in saggezza*, Milan, Gribaudi, 2001, 46.

[195] Emmanuel Lévinas, *L'aldilà del versetto*, Tr.it., Naples, Guida, 1986, 203; on this point see also William Schniedewind, *Come la Bibbia divenne un libro*, Brescia, Queriniana, 2008, 34 (*How the Bible Became a Book: The Textualization of Ancient Israel*, Cambridge, Cambridge University Press, 2015) and Michael Satlow, *E il Signore parlò a Mosé. Come la Bibbia divenne sacra*, Turin, Bollati e Boringhieri, 2015, 14.

[196] The story of the redaction of the Bible is very complex; alongside certainties there remain many open questions and hypotheses still to be proven or cast aside. Those who wish to explore the subject more deeply may consult extensive available bibliographies.

[197] Of the 46 books of the Hebrew Bible, only 24 are accepting in the biblical canon as the word of God, while the other 22 are considered edifying texts which must have been inserted into the first complete version of the Bible in Greek, redacted in the 3rd century BCE in Alexandria and known as the Septuagint (Seventy) after the number of translators that tradition holds to have been summoned

to translate the Hebrew text. These texts are not included in the canon of some Christian Protestant denominations. Cfr. Piero Stefani, *La Bibbia*, Bologna, il Mulino, 2004.

[198] The Pentateuch includes Genesis, Exodus, Leviticus, Numbers, and Deuteronomy..

[199] On the history of the text of the Bible see William M. Schniedewind, *Come la Bibbia divenne un libro*, cit. (*How the Bible Became* cit.); Jean Louis Ska, Daniel Attinger, *Un Dio che si implica nella nostra storia: una lettura del libro della Genesi*, a course conducted at Bose Monastery, ed. Qiqajon, in pdf.

[200] In every social group there were individuals whose task was to memorize and teach the history of the tribe or clan. The ancients trusted memory over the written word, which was long limited to practical matters (administration and economics), also because inscribing on stone was extremely labor intensive and the resulting objects were hard to transport. For the most part only the essential data of wars and conquests were incised on *stele*. As with all innovations, the invention of writing also provoked diffidence and hostility, not only because it appeared to threaten the power of an influential class, but also for fear it would weaken people's memory and lead to the loss of the stories entrusted to oral tradition.

[201] Piero Stefani, *La Bibbia*, cit., 13.

[202] People became slaves principally due to debt, and remained in servitude until they paid the debt off, according to agreement between debtor and creditor. The slave/servant became part of the master's household and shared its life; once the debt was paid, the slave might return to freedom or continue to work for the master on a salary.

[203] Cfr. Chaim Potok, *Storia degli Ebrei*, Milan, Garzanti, 2003 (*Chaim Potok's History of the Jews*, New York, Knopf, 1978).

[204] Exodus was probably redacted in the post-exilic period in Jerusalem, but it narrates events that are thought to have taken place around 1300-1200 BCE. It seems prudent to allow for a margin of doubt. Some research, in particular that of Italian archeologist Emmanuel Anati, could date the events narrated retroactively by several centuries. On the basis of his long, thoroughly annotated archeological work, Anati hypothesized that the sacred place referred to in Exodus, where Israel experienced a divine epiphany, was the site of Har Karkom in the Sinai peninsula, near the border between Israel and Egypt. He offers an appealing and convincing reconstruction, although he confuses some dates fixed by tradition.

[205] KJV, Exodus 20,2 and Deuteronomy 5,6; the version in Deuteronomy is the most ancient.

[206] In biblical Hebrew, the same word, *'eved*, signifies slave and servant..

[207] Michael Walzer, *Esodo e rivoluzione*, Milan, Feltrinelli, 1986, 16-17 (*Exodus and Revolution*, New York, Basic Books, 1986).

[208] *Ibidem*, 53-54.

[209] Moni Ovadia, *Vai a te stesso*, Turin, Einaudi, 2002, 25.

[210] Cfr. Emmanuel Lévinas, *Difficile libertà*, Brescia, La Scuola, 2000 (*Difficult Freedom: Essays on Judaism*, Baltimore, Johns Hopkins University Press, 1997).

[211] This is the fundamental thesis of Exodus, according to Michael Walzer, *Esodo e rivoluzione*, cit., 72-73.

[212] Cfr. Exodus 24, 7. The verse is often translated: "All that the Lord hath said we will do, and be obedient," but the literal translation is, "we will do and we will listen."

[213] KJV, Deuteronomy 5, 12-15: "Keep the sabbath day to sanctify it, as the Lord they God hath commanded thee. Six days thou shalt labour, and do all thy work: But the seventh day is the sabbath

of the Lord thy God: in it thous shalt not do any work, thou, nor thy son, nor thy daughter, nor thy manservant, nor thy maidservant, nor thine ox, nor thine ass, nor any of thy cattle, nor thy stranger that is within thy gates; that they manservant and they maidservant may rest as well as thou. And remember that thou wast a servant in the land of Egypt, and that the Lord thy God brought thee out thence through a mighty hand and by a stretched out arm: therefore the Lord thy God commanded thee to keep the sabbath holy."

Genesis 2, 2-3: "And on the seventh day God ended his work which he had made; and he rested on the seventh day from all his work which he had made. And God blessed the seventh day and sanctified it: because thaty in it he had rested from all his work which God created and made." On the meaning of sabbath, see also Abraham Heschel, *Il sabato*, Milan, Garzanti, 1999 (*The Sabbath. Its Meaning for Modern Man*, New York, Farrar Straus & Giroux, 1951).

[214] This intention is repeated in the biblical institution of the jubilee, the year of grace and liberation during which, every fifty years, slaves must be freed and justice restored, in the form of a right relation with things, other people, God, and nature. The sovereignty of God and his infinite freedom are made manifest in the liberation of every living thing and the land from any servitude.

[215] There is truly an abyss between the Greek heroes of Homer and the biblical heroes, who are so human, fragile, often insecure and scared, but who perform great actions not because they are great men but unwillingly, almost forced by God's will to act against their own wishes.

[216] On the meaning of the name of God, see Luigi Pareyson, *Ontologia della libertà*, cit., 122 sgg.

[217] Historically, the two words used in the Bible to speak of God define two differente ras: in the first, corresponding to the period of the patriarchs (ca. 1800-1200) God is identified as el/elohim/ of the Fathers, of Abraham, of Isaac, of Jacob. El (235 occurrences in the Old Testament) is a common word among Semitic peoples, of uncertain etymology, but probably comes from a root that signifies strength. It is the generic term to describe Semitic divinities, but also a specific god among the Canaanites: the king/father of the gods. The second era begins with the revelation to Moses on Mount Oreb, when the name of God becomes the tetragrammaton.

[218] Cfr. Daniel Attinger, *Un Dio che si implica nella nostra storia: una lettura del libro della Genesi*, cit., pdf.; Pietro Lombardini, *Il Dio di Mosè, Cuore di Dio, cuore dell'uomo*, Bologna, EDB, 2011.

[219] Luigi Pareyson, *Ontologia della libertà*, cit., 129-130.

[220] He proclaims his existence: I am that which is; this especially in the Greek tradition, which reflects the typically Greek philosophical and metaphysical concept of God as Being or That Which Is.

[221] "He is present and wants to be present due to his most intimate essence: as he who liberates, and can and wants to lead from death to life." Cfr. Erich Zenger, *Il Dio dell'Esodo*, Bologna, EDB, 1983.

[222] André Chouraqui, *Il mio testamento. Il fuoco dell'alleanza*, Brescia, Queriniana, 2002., 33. Continuing, he adds: "The fact that the tetragrammaton . . . is born from a root that means "to be" should inspire us and lead us to a unitary and multiform concept of the world." *Ivi*, 115-116.

[223] Gen 1-3: the creation in the garden of Eden; 4-12, stories of the first descendants of Adam and Eve. Beginning in chapter 12 come the stories of a specific Semitic group. On the interpretation and the story of Genesis and these chapters in particular, see, among other sources, Pietro Bovati, *Parole di libertà*, Bologna, EDB, 2012; and Daniel Attinger, *Un Dio che si implica nella nostra storia: una lettura del libro della Genesi*, cit.

[224] Cfr. Moni Ovadia, *Vai a te stesso*, cit.

[225] Hannah Harendt maintained that Christianity had been "truly the decisive factor" in the history of freedom because it taught mankind about internal freedom. Hannah Arendt, "What is Freedom?, in *Tra passato e futuro*, Milan, Garzanti 1991, 110-111 (*Between Past and Future*, London, Penguin, 2006).

[226] "Idolatry is nothing but the cultural form of tyranny. . . the gesture of breaking the idols that Abraham carries out [when he leaves Ur] is a gesture that defeats, on the level of thought, tribalism and the tyrannical forms of power based on force." Moni Ovadia, *Vai a te stesso*, cit., 15-16.

[227] Cfr. Pietro Bovati, "Libertà e liberazione nell'Antico Testamento", in *Dizionario di Spiritualità Biblico-Patristica, Libertà e liberazione nella Bibbia*, n.36, Borla, 2003.

[228] Daniel Attinger says that the first chapters of Genesis are in a certain sense conclusive: after the experience of God, Israel concludes that it is he who has created us.

[229] The plural *Elohim*, possibly derived from *El* (see previous footnote), indicated a superlative, thus the importance and greatness of this divinity: *Elohim* is the God of gods, he of whom there is none greater. For Christians this relates also to the idea of divine nature as relation and communion.

[230] André Chouraqui, *Il mio testamento*, cit., 11.

[231] Exegetes point out the interesting detail that when the serpent tempts Eve, he asks her whether it is true that they may neither *touch* the tree nor eat of it. He thus slyly induces the woman to converse with him, to explain to him that God had not told them they cannot touch it, but only that they cannot eat its fruit. Spiritual observers notice this as a scheme the demon employs to draw her into dialogue with him, as she believes she is simply helping the serpent to understand the command of God.

Notes to the Conclusion

[232] Luigi Pareyson, *Ontologia della libertà*, cit., 224.

[233] *Ibidem*, 465.

[234] Cfr Freeman Dyson, *Turbare l'universo*, Turin, Bollati Boringhieri, 1999 (*Disturbing the Universe*, cit.).

[235] Cfr. John Polkinghorne, *Scienza e Provvidenza*, cit. (*Science and Providence*, cit.).

[236] Carlo Rovelli, *Reality is Not What It Seems. The Journey to Quantum Gravity*, trans. by Simon Carnell & Erica Segre, New York, Riverhead, 2017, 135 (cfr. *La realtà non è come ci appare*, cit., 118).

[237] "Il Sole 24 ore" March 30, 2014.

[238] ". . . contemporary scientific theories interact with philosophy in two directions. On one hand, confirmed scientific theories have notable repercussions on traditionally 'philosophical' problems, as demonstrated for example by the impact of Darwinian evolution on traditional questions about the origin of human beings, or even our moral rules. On the other hand, in what is technically called the 'interpretation' of a scientific or physical theory—which is the attempt to understand what that theory tells us about reality or the world—it is indispensable to use the instruments of conceptual analysis provided by philosophy in an appropriate way. It was thanks to an attentive philosophical analysis of the meaning of 'a is simultaneous with b' (when this relation is attributed to events far distant from one another) that Einstein was able to constitute his theory of Special Relativity." Mauro Dorato, *Cosa c'entra l'anima con gli atomi?*, Bari, Laterza 2007 (digital edition, 2015, position 301).

[239] Vito Mancuso, *Il principio passione*, cit., 192.

[240] Luigi Pareyson, *Ontologia della libertà*, 135.

[241] Carlo Rovelli, *Reality is Not What It Seems*, cit., 129 (*La realtà*, cit, 114).

[242] Christian De Duve, *Da Gesù a Gesù passando per Darwin*, Milan, Edizioni San Paolo, 2013, 66.

[243] Translation by Ulrich Schaffer: https://www.cloisterseminars.org/blog/2017/12/31/by-gracious-powers-wonderfully-sheltered-a-blessing-for-the-turn-of-the-year

Acknowledgments

It is a pleasurable duty to thank those who, in various ways, have contributed to this work: Luigi Maramotti, Annamaria Tagliavini, Thomas Haskell Simpson, Marco Belpoliti, Andrea Chiarenza, Matteo Galaverni, Telmo Pievani, Annamaria Fabbi, Annamaria Fulloni, Mariangela Barchi, Laura Artioli, Ugo Berti, Franco Nasi. My sincere gratitude to all.

Books published by Agincourt Press

Mariano Bàino, *Yellow Fax and Other Poems* (2019)

Alfredo Giuliani (ed.), *I Novissimi* (2017)

Gianluca Rizzo (ed.), *On the Fringe of the Neoavantgarde / Ai confine della neoavanguardia, Palermo 1963 – Los Angeles 2013* (2017)

Massimo Ciavolella and Gianluca Rizzo (ed.), *Savage Words: Invectives as a Literary Genre* (2016)

Massimo Ciavolella and Gianluca Rizzo (ed.), *Like Doves Summoned by Desire: Dante's New Life in 20th Century Literature and Cinema. Essays in memory of Amilcare Iannucci* (2012)

Elio Pagliarani, *The Girl Carla and Other Poems* (2009)

Maurizio Cucchi, *The Missing* (2008)

Remo Bodei, *We, The Divided: Ethos, Politics, and Culture in Post-War Italy, 1943-2006* (2006)

Standard Shaefer, *Water & Power* (2005)

Robert Crosson, *The Day Sam Goldwyn Stepped off the Train* (2004)

Paul Vangelisti, *Embarrassment of Survival* (2001)